Can God Come to Work with Me?

Encouraging Devotions to Strengthen Christians in the Secular Workplace

Dr. Wendy J. Flint, PhD

Edited by Twylla Koehler

Can God Come to Work with Me?

Encouraging Devotions to Strengthen Christians in the Secular Workplace

USA ISBN 978-0-9818470-2-3
Word Unlimited

All scripture passages are from the NIV Version of the Bible unless otherwise noted.

The Podcasts "Can God Come to Work with Me?" have a few word differences than the book.

Printed in the United States of America

Word Unlimited Publishing
Since 1985
Sherwood, OR
Contact information updated @ **www.wendyflint.com**

Dedication

I dedicate this book to Jesus who taught me about the power of love and forgiveness and how to navigate Biblical values in daily leadership and decision making.

"Jesus said to him, "You shall love the Lord your God with all your heart and with all your soul and with all your mind. This is the great and first commandment. And a second is like it: You shall love your neighbor as yourself."

Matthew 22:37 - 39

Preface

With years of corporate and public-school experience, I have maturely come to realize that opportunities to openly share the gospel of Christ in the secular workplace is very limited. Until recently, it could even bring on a religious lawsuit, particularly in public sector organizations.

The "anti-Christian" pressures in the workplace and lawsuits in the news the past 25 years, have caused people of faith to shut down and separate their religion from their work. In 2015, a high school football coach, Kennedy, lost his job for taking a knee to pray AFTER every game in the center of the field. No students were required to attend.

In June 2022, the Supreme Court ruled that this went against Kennedy's 1st Amendment Rights – freedom of speech and freedom of religion. Going forward, there could be less pressure on Christians, as our freedoms are being recognized and restored.

Like Daniel in the Bible, Kennedy refused to comply and embraced his Constitutional right to pray.

In 2017, a Southwest Airlines flight attendant posted on her personal social media that she was pro-life. She was fired for posting a political point of view that was part of her religious values. She filed a lawsuit against the company and the union.

In 2022, A federal jury in Texas sided with the former Southwest flight attendant, arguing that she was unlawfully discriminated against for her sincerely held religious beliefs. Furthermore, the jury found that the union did not fairly represent her and retaliated against her for expressing her views. She was awarded 5.3 million.

Taking God to work with us does not mean we preach or force our beliefs on others. It does mean we have the freedom to have our own religious point of view without persecution.

This book is not about our Constitutional Rights. Rather it is about how we can bring His love into the workplace and how we can depend on God to help us with decisions and work relationships.

"Marketplace Christianity" means integrating God in our daily lives, in our leadership, through our decision making, and mostly through our acts of kindness. It further means, trusting God for wisdom and strength in work assignments and demonstrating excellence and integrity as a representative of His kingdom.

Oswald Chambers, author of My Utmost for His Highest, understood this kind of Christianity. Oswald wrote:

> "There are not three levels of spiritual life – worship, waiting, and work. God's idea is that the three should go together as one. They were always together in the life of our Lord and in perfect harmony. It is a discipline that must be developed; it will not happen overnight." (Chambers, 1992).

Billy Graham said, "I believe one of the next great moves of God will happen through the believers in the workplace." Many Christians ponder how this can happen.

With church attendance at an all-time low with Millennials and Gen Z, our hope to reach the next generation of faith-based leaders, is through our relationships in the workplace.

> *"I believe one of the next great moves of God will happen through the believers in the workplace."*
> **Billy Graham**

The stories in these devotions will demonstrate how this happens through a daily experience where your work life and spiritual life joyfully intersect.

Table of Contents

Introduction

Many years ago, during a quiet prayer time, I heard in my spirit a question from the Lord. Having conversations with God in my heart and head has been a normal part of my life since I received Jesus as my Savior at age 23. I don't know any other way to walk with Him except in prayer conversations.

The Lord asked me: "Would you be willing to go through some challenging experiences so you could be empathetic with others and know better how to encourage and pray for them?" My response was, "Will it be very painful?"

He replied, "Yes – but I will make every experience short-lived until you get a 'faith understanding' for the situation. I will be with you always." I'm never able to say "no" to the Lord, because I love Him more than life.

We had an agreement and He asked me to write everything down that I learned. I have dozens of journals and I love fancy pens. Writing became my lifestyle. I work for a living, but I write for joy.

I didn't realize at the time, but it gradually became evident that most of "my experiences" were going to be in the workplace. I suffered trials of controlling supervisors, verbally abusive managers, jealous or mean coworkers, jobs where I was ignored and unappreciated, layoffs, mergers, a religious lawsuit, and company corruption.

There were some breaks in the journey where I was empowered and joyful, had good managers; but that was short-lived. God wanted to show me the unhappiness of people in their careers and how everyday was a struggle for most employees.

He wanted me to overcome the challenges through faith, so I could encourage others to allow God to walk with them in the workplace and trust Him in all circumstances – or in some cases, pursue an education and seek new opportunities.

No wonder we just experienced "the great resignation" in 2021 and 2022, following the pandemic, with millions resigning or changing jobs, seeking joy in their careers or at minimum – life-work balance. People started questioning, "Why should I be unhappy in my employment?"

There is a new phenomenon going on called "flight risk of high performers." Companies are figuring out the algorithms of when an employee will jump ship. Human Resource departments are training managers to recognize and reward high performers to improve retention rates.

Could it be that a new era of compassionate managers is on the horizon? As long as human nature is not operating in the fruits of the spirit or what the world calls emotional intelligence, it may be a long time coming.

These devotions were written over a period of time through several jobs, but many were never published until now. As I reviewed many of the messages, I realized that I was still waiting for some dreams to come to pass, even though many of the messages are encouraging the readers to have hope in the promised vision.

I asked the Lord, "What should I say to people who are thinking, 'Why should I believe her? Her calling has still not come to pass?' How do I explain that some of your promises to me were 25 to 30 years ago?"

He said, "Tell them that Abraham and Sara were 90 years old when their promise of a son came to pass. Tell them you prayed for your mother to be saved for 45 years before that prayer was answered. Tell them that Caleb waited 40 years and he was 85 years old before he finally went into the promise land. Tell them that from the time you were "on the tarmac" (devotion #15) until now (15 years), you have gained extreme amounts of training and wisdom. You have grown leaps and bounds in your faith. You have been prepared for such a time as this. Tell them, the vision will not be one day late."

I am also reminded, that if the vision came to pass swiftly and easily, we would be tempted to take the glory for our gifts and talents When it seems impossible, God gets the glory.

Devotion #1: Run with Horses

"If you have run with footmen, and they have wearied you, then how can you contend with horses? And if in the land of peace, in which you trusted, they wearied you, then how will you do in the floodplain of the Jordan?" (Jeremiah 12:5)

Jeremiah, an Old Testament prophet, was given the task of warning the people to get their act right with God. After a few attempts with no success, he complained to God about the people. God responded: with the message about horses. "If you can't run with people – how will you run with horses?"

In other words, God had a big plan for Jeremiah, and he needed to allow the circumstances and people prepare him. When I have differences at work with people, I often think of this scripture verse. I even have a painting of horses in my office.

The scripture also indicates that if you can't handle challenges in "peaceful" times; what will you do during food shortages, inflation, high gas prices, or the threat of oppressive political leaders?

What God is saying is, if we can't pass the test with small challenges and personality conflicts, we are not ready for greater leadership responsibility. The same is true in our service to the Lord.

If we are not being faithful in the little things or managing the level of finances He has given us, then we are not ready for the increase or the bigger vision.

God has chosen us for an assignment, but in order to qualify us, He puts us in situations to prepare us for what He wants us to achieve. Our spiritual growth and our physical responsibilities with work, family, community, and church are very integrated.

God's ultimate goal for us is to "run and not be weary" and to bear the fruits of the spirit in the face of a complaining generation. The higher up on the management ladder you go, the more personalities and differences of opinion you will experience.

Give each day and each situation to the Lord and allow each challenge to become a new step of strength in your life. Soon you'll be riding on the horses and across the floodplains, and it will seem easy because the Lord has groomed you for the task.

For a practical application, using your strengths will make you more motivated in your job and increase energy and productivity and equip you to handle challenges. If you don't know your strengths, I recommend going to Clifton Strengths Finder located on the web at **strengthsquest.com**.

I am a certified strengths coach, and I consider this an important step in discovering the gifts and talents God gave you. It's worth the investment of a small fee to take the test and read the report.

I encourage you to leverage your strengths in each situation and delegate out assignments that are not your strengths.

Prayer

Lord,

We thank you for the challenging circumstances and people in our lives that grows our character and increases the fruit in our lives of long suffering, love, kindness, and joy. We ask that you give us grace, wisdom, and strength to endure workplace challenges and prepare us for our calling where we will run with horses. Help us to discover the gifts and strengths you have given us so that we may give to others.

In Jesus' name, Amen.

Devotion #2: My Dog ZuZu

"Behold, God is my helper and ally; the Lord is my upholder and is with them who uphold my life." (Psalms 54:4, Amplified)

We had a dog named ZuZu. At age 5-years old, he went completely blind. We didn't let him in the backyard in California unless we were home because of the swimming pool.

We had pool-trained all our dogs – taking them in the water and showing them where the steps are located.

When ZuZu fell in, he knew that the steps were there – but not sure where. He would calmly follow the edge of the pool, all the way around, paddling until his feet hit the steps. Sometimes I would jump in to rescue him – but usually, he was on his way out of the water by the time I reached him.

This was an amazing feat for this breed of dog – short of a miracle – because Chinese Shar-peis typically can't swim. Their heads are too big and their feet too small – so they eventually sink. God gave ZuZu big feet – so he was equipped to survive.

I think we can take a lesson from ZuZu. If he had panicked and tried to pull his wet body out of the edge of the pool where he fell– he would have become exhausted and given up. Instead, he stayed calm, and by "faith" and memory of the promise that there were steps, he kept going forward. After a couple of times of success – learning that the steps would indeed always be there – he found his way more quickly to the path of safety.

Even if we are barely treading water – if we move toward our goal, we will eventually reach it. If we stay calm and focused – keeping our spiritual eyes fixed on God's promises – we will find our way out of every situation. If we panic – we may miss the path to success. Yes, God will come to the rescue – but in the end – He wants us to learn to trust what He has promised and keep putting one foot in front of the other.

It did not give me joy to see ZuZu suffer from his blindness, but it did give me joy to see how carefully God cared for him and I too can trust He will care for me.

Have there been times in your career where you feel you were swimming blind and not sure where you were headed? How did it turn out? Recalling what God did for us in the past gives us assurance for our future.

A practical idea is to meditate or write down the times God rescued you and record how everything turned out just fine. If you are waiting for a breakthrough in your job, career, or vision – what actions can you take to not panic and keep swimming?

By the way, you will be happy to know that when we moved to Texas, we had a home with no pool and ZuZu joyfully ran around the yard until it was his time to crossover to heaven.

Prayer

Lord,

Sometimes it's hard to put our trust in you when we can't see the future. I guess that is why they call it "blind-faith." In times of uncertainty, please give us peace and calm to keep on swimming until we reach our destination. Show us practical and prayerful things we can do while we are waiting. Thank you for your promise in Jeremiah 29:11 which says you "know the plans you have for us and for our future and they are for good and not for evil."

In Jesus' name, Amen.

Devotion #3: The Same Wind

"All things work together for good to them that love God, to them who are the called according to his purpose." (Romans 8:28)

The Bible dictionary says that finding favor means gaining approval, acceptance, or special benefits. One evening while watching TV with my husband, I asked, "Why does the favor on my jobs keep changing?"

I did not have favor at my last job – in fact, I was disrespected as a woman in leadership and prevented from using my talents. I worked hard for business sales, and I prayed for blessings on the programs that I ran – but the success was minimal.

In my current job, I applied the same marketing and sales principles (and prayers) and I had extreme favor and success for three years. But now, sales are down, and I struggle once again with favor.

I asked, "Since I have not changed in my walk with God – what makes the difference?" He replied that he didn't know.

We changed the channel and there was a famous pastor teaching. He shared how he was jogging one day, and a wind came up against him. It was so strong, that he could hardly run, and it was exhausting.

He did not think he could do one more lap and was about to quit. He turned the corner, and the wind was now at his back. It was pushing him along and he completed in this goal time to the finish line.

He then made this profound statement: "The wind of adversity in your life will become the same wind that carries you to the finish line if you persevere and trust God." My husband turned to me and said,

> "There's your answer. Your last job actually prepared you for this job. In fact, you would not have this job if you had not worked at your former location, and you would not have been prepared for the high pressures of this job which led to success. Perhaps what you are going through right now is again preparing you for something greater in the future."

The wisdom of this has helped me for many years. On a practical note, journaling your experiences is an excellent way to see God's plan and preparation on your path to higher places.

As you look back on your reflections and prayers in your journal, you will see a pattern of challenge, struggle, prayer, trust, breakthrough, and finally new beginnings. Writing down God's answers to prayer, gives us hope for our future when we need it most.

Prayer

Lord,

In those times when things are not going right and it feels like we have lost your favor, help us to remember all the times you did answer prayer. Help us to trust and believe that all things truly do work together for good for those who trust you and are called according to Your purpose.

In Jesus' name, Amen.

Devotion #4: Pressing On – Pressing In

"We are hard-pressed on every side, yet not crushed; we are perplexed, but not in despair; persecuted, but not forsaken; struck down, but not destroyed." (2 Corinthians 4:6-7)

There are certain times in history when one generation believes they dealt with more pressure than the previous generation. My parents and grandparents were survivors of the Great Depression and World War II, and they thought my generation was extremely blessed.

My husband and I are Veterans who served during the Vietnam War, and we saw the suffering of families who lost their young sons and daughters, so we had our own pressures in the 60s.

The truth is that people today have their own levels of pressure and anxiety. We deal with new technology, workplace pressures, single parenting, inflation, high mortgages, and pandemics, to name a few.

Apostle Paul wrote a great deal about how to endure the pressures of the world, and he reminds us that even in difficult times we can always sense God's sustainability in our lives.

When Paul pleaded with the Lord to make Satan stop persecuting him and to remove the thorn in his flesh, the Lord said: "My grace is sufficient for you, for my strength is made perfect in weakness" (2 Corinthians 12:9).

Paul told the Christ followers, "I take pleasure in infirmities, in reproaches, in needs, in persecutions, in distresses, for Christ's sake. For when I am weak, then I am strong" (V. 10).

We must remember that it is not always about us – it's about God's glory *in* us. The pressure in our life releases God's glory for others to see.

So, what are we to do under pressure? We are to *press on* and *press in*. We press on to finish the task God has called us, to pursue the dream we have in our hearts, and run the race to the finish line. To receive strength, we are to press into Jesus, and He will give us the ability and grace to endure as we run the race.

Executive coach, John Maxwell wrote about Apostle Paul's thorn in the flesh:

> "Instead of getting angry at his thorn (weakness) and the way it slowed him down, Paul relished how weak it made him. Why? It kept him in close dependence on the power of God. Paul understood that the weaker he was, the stronger God became within him. When there is less of you as a leader, there is more of God as the Leader."

As leaders, we often feel inadequate or overwhelmed at challenges or major decisions we have to make. We question our call to leadership. But it's in those moments we can rejoice in our weakness because we can have the assurance that God's strength and wisdom in us is greater than what we can do on our own.

Prayer

Lord,

Someone reading this right now is feeling like they want to give up on the job position you have given them. They are growing weary and want to throw in the towel. But you are saying to him or her right now, "lean on me and let me be strong in your weakness." I release your peace and presence into that person's life right now and I pray that you will give your children who are serving you in the workplace what they need to continue, to succeed, and to run the race to the finish line.

In Jesus's Name, Amen.

Devotion #5: Cowboy Wisdom

"I know that nothing is better for them than to rejoice and to do good in their lives, and also that every man should eat and drink and enjoy the good of all his labor – it is the gift of God." (Ecclesiastes 3:12-13)

When we lived in Texas, I had paintings of horses and cowboys. In a painting of a cattle drive, the cattle are not walking, but rather grazing in the pasture, as the cowboy sits on his horse overseeing and protecting.

With my personality style, I would rather have the cattle running with my horse going at a nice trot next to them. The Lord was trying to give me a message through the painting that "not stampeding" can be a good thing.

I researched cowboys and found that cattle drives had to strike a balance between speed and the weight of the cattle. While cattle could be driven 25 miles a day, they would lose so much weight they couldn't be sold at the end of the trail.

By going shorter distances each day, the cattle were allowed to rest and graze twice a day. Maintaining a slow pace meant that it took two months to travel from a ranch to a railroad station, as some trails were 1,000 miles long.

Perhaps if we had a clear understanding of why the Lord has us travel at a slower pace at times, we could better endure the wait for the end goal we are hoping will come. Here are a few good reasons why the Lord wants us to pace our lives:

1. If we go too fast, we could miss a new course of direction that He is trying to steer us toward (no pun intended).
2. If we don't pace ourselves, we may not want to stop on the trail to minister to someone the Lord brings in our path. (We'll use the excuse we are in a hurry).
3. If we don't schedule stopping points, we will be worn out at the end of the trail.
4. Feeding on the Word of the Lord along the way for nourishment and direction is what the Lord intends.
5. Slowness in one area of our life allows us to spend time in another area that we normally are too busy to attend. (I learned that the cowboys wrote lots of songs and poetry!)
6. We need to enjoy the fruit of our labor – not just focus on the labor.
7. We need to be obedient because the Lord is also watching out for our safety, and He knows best what lies ahead.

On a practical thought in the business world, going with the flow and pacing ourselves is a "change skill" that corporations are looking for in employees. It's called "flexibility" or "adaptability." Instead of stressing and complaining about the slow down and waiting situations, we need recognize it's time to graze.

Prayer

Lord,

Help us to not get ahead of ourselves and make quick decisions to fill in a slow gap. Instead, let us slow down and thoughtfully pray and wait on you for next steps. Let us be aware of our surroundings and be present in the moment so we are available to minister to others, take care of our families, and enjoy life.

In Jesus' name, Amen.

Devotion #6: You Are Not Camping

"Thus, says the Lord of hosts, the God of Israel, to all who were carried away captive, who I have caused to be carried away from Jerusalem to Babylon: Build houses and dwell in them; plant gardens and eat their fruit. Take wives and have sons and daughters . . .that you may be increased there, and not diminished." (Jeremiah 29:4-6)

When the Israelites went into captivity in Babylon, they were waiting for a message from the prophet Jeremiah who was still in Jerusalem. They were hoping for a message from God that said, "Keep your bags packed – you're coming back soon."

Instead, they were given a message that said they were going to be in Babylon for a while, so they needed to make the best of it.

The letter from Jeremiah was suggesting: "You are not on a camping trip. This is your new home. Develop your community. Be productive. Cultivate where you are. Remember, their welfare is your welfare. Make the best of it. Find God in your current circumstances. Build houses. Grow gardens. Get married and have children."

God is telling us through this story that we need to "bloom where we are planted." We need to be productive and cultivate our skills. We also need to pray for our workplace and community because as Jeremiah said, "their peace is our peace" (Jeremiah 29:7).

What a powerful message that promotes the concept "God is Lord of business and the marketplace." God wants us to continue to serve and trust Him in our place of employment and in difficult situations.

Along with the discouraging message "be happy in your captivity" – Jeremiah also prophesied hope for the final outcome. In fact, a favorite and frequently quoted scripture is in this letter sent to Babylon: "For I know the thoughts that I think toward you, says the Lord, thoughts of peace and not of evil, to give you a future and a hope." (Jeremiah 29:11).

The situation was not to be forever, but in the meantime, they needed to get on with the normalcy of life. God's people were told that in 70 years they would be brought out of Babylon and returned to their homeland – and it happened just as promised.

Do you feel like you are in a captivity in your job and wish you could move on? The "Babylon workplace experiences" do not last forever. God always has a plan for good and for your future.

A practical idea is to make a list of the "good things" you are getting from your work experience. Reflect on all the skills you have learned and opportunities you have experienced over the past year or two. Now that you have marked, acknowledged, and appreciated this stage in your life, don't be surprised if the next path and journey is just around the corner. I promise – it won't be 70 years.

Prayer

Lord,

Sometimes our job isn't what we were hoping for. Right now, many of us are lacking joy. As we are waiting or seeking for that job that fits us perfectly and uses our gifts and talents, help us to have joy in you. Help us to have hope in our future. We believe and declare that you have a plan for us, and we trust your word is true.

In Jesus' name, Amen.

Devotion #7: Passed Over

"For not from the east nor from the west nor from the south come promotion and lifting up, but God is the judge! He puts down one, and lifts up another." (Psalms 75:6-7)

I have been passed over many times in the church and the workplace. I have often felt invisible at team meetings. I have watched others who have not demonstrated integrity, morality or fruits of the Spirit get chosen for leadership.

It can be very painful and confusing – but since my trust is in the Lord and not in man – I have learned to be at peace and know that in due time He will exalt me. He will know when I am ready.

Once in the past when I did not get a promotion where had the highest qualifications and tenure, a co-worker said, "Are you upset? I can't believe they did not choose you. Everyone is talking about it and in shock."

I replied, "That is very sweet. I am a little disappointed and confused, but my personal faith assures me that 'man' can do nothing for me or against me that God does not approve in advance. I think He has a perfect plan for me and this was not the plan."

I love the story of Moses choosing the 70 elders to help him manage 600,000 men plus their wives and children. God came in a cloud and put the same Spirit that was on Moses on the elders. (Numbers 11:2-25).

The elders began to worship God and prophesy – declaring God's will. Back in the camp there were two men not chosen as elders – but the Spirit fell on them too and they were worshiping and prophesying. (Verses 26-28)

The people "tattled" and told Moses to stop them because "they were not chosen" – but Moses said, "I wish that *all* the Lord's people were prophets and that the Lord would put His Spirit on them." (Verse 29)

I have learned that you may be denied by men – but you will be declared by God and your gifts will come forth and be used in a mighty way in His time. I certainly can testify to that. Shortly later, I left this organization and was hired as a senior executive in another company with a pay increase of $30,000. The job that I didn't get, no longer exists.

Is there someone in the workplace that keeps getting a promotion and favor that you envy? Give it over to God in prayer and don't let the negative seed consume your heart.

What do you do in the meantime? Document all your successes and achievements and keep your resume up to date. Do your part to look for advancement in your current organization or job opportunities somewhere else. When the right door opens – step through.

Prayer

Lord,

Sometimes you want us to stay and learn a few more lessons and sometimes you want us to leave. Give us the grace to stay in challenging situations and the courage to seek new opportunities when it is time. When we are not sure what to do, help us to put our faith in You and trust that you have a perfect plan. Thank you for your provision. I am grateful for all you have done for me. Help me to be perceptive to your will.

In Jesus' name, Amen.

Devotion #8: Small Acts of Kindness

"For this very reason, make every effort to add to your faith goodness; and to goodness, knowledge; and to knowledge, self-control; and to self-control, perseverance; and to perseverance, godliness; and to godliness, brotherly kindness; and to brotherly kindness, love." (2 Peter 1:5-7)

One day I boarded an oversold and overcrowded flight to San Francisco. Everyone scrambled to stow their luggage in a coveted overhead bin.

I observed a woman who was one of the last ones to drag her luggage down the aisle as she worked her way toward the last stand-by seat in front of me.

She struggled with her small bag, computer, and coat as she spotted a small spot left in the bin. Everyone stared at her as she seemed to take longer than necessary to figure out where to put everything and get seated.

I jumped up and said, "Here, let me hold your things while you get your bag in place." She gratefully handed me her coat and computer and caught my eyes for a split second to say a quick "thank you."

I found a place for her coat, waited for her to slide into her seat between two others, then handed her the computer and got myself re-settled.

She turned around and said, "I really needed someone to be nice to me today. I've had a terrible morning and everyone has been so unkind. Your act of kindness really encouraged me. Thank you."

The word *kindness* sort of hung in the air around everyone as if to say – "See how easy that was everyone. Pay attention more to each other."

I thought, "That was so easy – has the world really become so busy, so selfish, or so unhappy, there is no time for kindness?" In that moment I understood the power of "a small act of kindness."

Jesus tells us to love our neighbor. Kindness is an action that demonstrates that love. We can impact our workplace and change the world one kindness at a time. As we spend time with God and His Word, we will grow in our peace in a stressful world. We can then be more aware of others and take the time to share God's love in small caring ways.

Prayer

Lord,

Forgive me for the times I was too busy to notice the needs of those around me. At work this week, show me who needs an encouraging word or a small act of kindness. I am available for you to use me.

In Jesus' name, Amen.

Devotion # 9: Lesson from a Horse

"Do not judge, or you too will be judged. For in the same way you judge others, you will be judged, and with the same measure you use, it will be measured to you." (Matthew 7:1)

My dream is to have a leadership conference center where horses (and other animals) are a part of the leadership learning experience.

On a flight to Maryland, I sat next to an airline captain on her way back from a horsemanship training center in California. I showed her pictures of my six grandchildren, and she showed me pictures of her three horses.

I asked her about horse training, and she said that every horse has a different motivation that you need to discover to get them to respond. They either want safety, comfort, water, food, or kudus. It is rare, but a few horses perform just for the praise.

It reminded me of Maslow's Theory of Hierarchy of Needs that explains why people work. The lowest motivation is to eat and survive and the highest motivation is for personal satisfaction of achievement.

The airline Captain shared that horses want to please you, but we can't communicate effectively with them, so we have to discover what works by trial and error. There are a lot of things a horse can't do for itself and it is dependent on the trainer for direction. Once the horse trusts the trainer, it is easier to communicate.

She went on to explain that when the horse finally understands, there is an actual sign of relief on the horse and a display of less stress, less resistance, and more confidence. I was amazed at how much this sounded like people that I managed.

This concept is similar to a leadership method called "situational leadership." In the beginning with a new employee or new assignment – more time needs to be spent on giving directions and ensuring that there is clarity in the communication. Through reward and recognition, the employee gradually moves in a direction of more independence and high performance.

Jesus was always asking people "What do you want me to do for you?" or asking His disciples, "What are you thinking right now about this?" Even though He had authority and power – He was always asking instead of telling – evaluating each situation.

This suggests some practical ideas for leaders. Think about your employees or team members as individuals. Find out what motivates them – what worries them – or why they took the job. Discover what their career goals are and pray about what you can do to help get them there. Good leaders motivate others by listening. Listen and then act on what you hear.

Currently I'm teaching management courses to Generation Z students. They tell me in class and in their assignments that they are really hoping for job satisfaction working for managers who listen to them, and they hope to be those kinds of leaders when they are promoted.

Prayer

Lord,

Help us as leaders to be willing to adapt to the needs of each generation and respond to each employee and colleague as an individual with unique needs. With your wisdom and your love, I know I can be a better leader and motivator. Help me to guide others gently and with patience the way you guide your children.

In Jesus name, Amen.

Devotion #10: I Know Your Voice

"Commit your works to the Lord, and your thoughts will be established. . . A man's heart plans his way, but the Lord directs his steps." (Proverbs 16: 3 & 9)

My adult daughter said to me, "Mom, when you leave a voicemail, you don't need to say 'this is mom' – I know your voice."

It made me think about the question, "How do you know God's voice?"

Part of knowing God's voice is knowing that the direction we are hearing in our hearts and minds aligns with the character of God. The character of God is full of peace, not stress or strife; the character of God is gentle, not forceful; and the character of God is having a sound mind, not confusion.

Direction and decisions that are of God are clear, concise, and full of peace – even in the midst of a crisis. You don't have to force yourself to go in the direction you are being guided in – you *know* that it is right.

I was asked by my students at Biola University if my direction and wisdom to make leadership decisions came from the Holy Spirit or from my education and training. I replied: "Both. God is a Spirit, but He is also a practical God who works through people – or he would not have used a construction manager (Nehemiah) to restore the wall in Jerusalem."

The way I see it, is the Holy Spirit combines the word of God and our faith with our experiences and practical knowledge, stirs it in a bowl, and it comes out *WISDOM*.

All the training, all the preparation, all the coaching and counseling from other leaders, all the reading of the Bible and business books, and all the praying, has been God's voice into my life because I TRUST that according to His word, He causes my thoughts to become agreeable to His will as I am making professional business decisions.

Proverbs 16:3 (Amplified) affirms: "Roll your works upon the Lord [commit and trust them wholly to Him; He will cause your thoughts to become agreeable to His will, and] so shall your plans be established and succeed."

Hearing God's voice and direction is most clear when we are reading the word and praying. This is how God comes to work with us. More and more, I am learning to invite him into my situation and give him a chance to work with me.

I get to work early to read my Bible and a daily devotion. I go for a walk on a break and spend time talking to him. And when I face a challenge, I ask him to show me what to do. He's always been faithful to answer that prayer through someone else, through something I read, or with a still small voice of direction.

Prayer

Lord,

Help us to understand that our mind and heart work together, along with your scriptures, for us to hear your voice and know Your direction. For my brothers and sisters who are seeking direction and answers to their questions, bring them a word through someone else, through something they read, and through quiet prayer. The Bible says You are not in the storm but rather You are in the quiet – You are a still small voice. Give us peace and help us to be quiet so we can hear your messages of guidance.

In Jesus name, Amen.

Devotion #11: Alert and Oriented Times 4

"He who dwells in the secret place of the Most High shall remain stable and fixed under the shadow of the Almighty whose power no foe can withstand." (Psalm 91:1)

Our middle son was trained as an EMT and a paramedic firefighter. There is a quick evaluation they do on the patient to determine if he or she is alert and to what level the patient is oriented. They do this by looking in the eyes and asking questions.

A normal person responding positive, is "Alert and Oriented Times 4." If the person cannot remember recent events, he or she is "Alert and Oriented Times 3." More disoriented – Times 2; drunk or in shock – Times 1; and a complete loss of identity of unconscious is "Alert and Oriented Times 0."

We can use this measurement in our own lives with our emotions or spiritual reactions. A crisis can take us to a "3," "2," or "1" in the form of depression, loss of hope, low self-esteem, heart ache, or grief. A "0" means a complete loss of our identity and who we are in Christ.

I think the Lord wants us to prepare to be "Alert and Oriented Times 4" in time of crisis. If we have proper preparation in the Word and spend time with God in daily prayer, we can quickly come back around during an emergency.

When our son takes a firefighter test, demonstrating his paramedic skills in front of a panel of evaluators, he finds himself in a state of "3" or "2" from the stress. He performs accurately, but he has occasionally been too slow and has to re-take the test.

However, in a REAL emergency on the job – everything always comes together for him. He is alert, accurate, fast, and saves lives. All his training and preparation produces a "4." Part of it is the adrenaline, but most of it is his focus on the person and years of experience and training.

In time of crisis, like adrenaline, the Holy Spirit will guide us – but we also need to be equipped and prepared – even if we must re-take the test. Preparation comes with Word of God training – no other way. But we can remain "Alert and Oriented Times 4" if we "fix our eyes not on what is seen but on what is unseen." (2 Corinthians 4:18)

In time of crisis at home or at work, you can give into your emotions of panic and fear, or you can train yourself to lean into God and draw from His strength, proclaiming His Word in the situation.

At the time of this writing, we have just come through over two years of a pandemic and we are entering an economic crisis. I think our training has prepared us for other challenges in the future. A lot of people are going to depend on our calm, our peace, our prayers, and our comfort. We need to stay ready and Alert and Oriented Times 4.

Prayer

Lord,

For all those reading, I pray they have been encouraged to stay in the Word and keep their eyes on you to prepare for any crisis. Continue to grow our faith and ready us for the days ahead where we can bring your love and blessing to others who are disoriented.

In Jesus name, Amen.

Devotion #12: Bluetooth Generation

"In a multitude of words, transgression is not lacking, but he who restrains his lips is prudent. The tongue of those who are upright and in right standing with God is as choice silver; the mind of those who are wicked and out of harmony with God is of little value." (Proverbs 10:19 & 20, Amplified).

I used to travel frequently, and I would be in two to four airports a month, sometimes every week. It was commonplace to see business people sitting in the gate area talking to "no one." They were actually conducting business through their wireless phone earpiece – called a *Bluetooth*.

Almost every trip, there was a man pacing the floor and yelling at his girlfriend or wife about some detail that didn't get done or some attitude that he didn't like. Sometimes a business woman is yelling at a staff member. It always troubled me.

Everyone in the waiting area cringes and feels sorry for the person at the other end of his or her wrath. We sort of eye one another in amazement that someone actually talks this way to another human being and gets away with it.

I asked myself – what could make a sane, normal human being act this way? Could it be a missed flight, jet lag, financial stress to name a few? Or is it perhaps a controlling nature that is frustrated being away from home and losing control?

The workplace is becoming more and more stressful with shorter deadlines, fast paced decisions, and economic downfalls. I think the anger I saw in the airport is the result of the world's pressure for financial success.

If stress and anger destroy your peace, joy, family life and work relationships, then the prosperity and success you are trying to attain is actually making you poor.

We must keep God's perspective in these high-pressured times. I believe when we meet our Maker, God will not ask how much money we made or what company we created – but He will rather ask, "How did you love?" How did you love the family and friends I gave you? How did you love others in your neighborhood or workplace?

As Jesus perfectly explains in Matthew 6:19-21: "Do not gather and heap up for yourselves treasures on earth, where moth and rust does corrupt, and where thieves break through and steal; but gather and heap up and store for yourselves treasures in heaven . . . For where your treasure is, there will you heart be also."

Do you use high pressure and stress as an excuse to be temperamental or unkind to someone? Instead of rationalizing or yielding over to self-indulging behavior, reflect on God's way of dealing with it and give the pressure over to Him. Trust God that if you put "first things first" in your behavior that everything else will be taken care of and fall in to place.

A practical idea I share with students during the *Time and Stress Management* training, is viewing a short 5-minute video on YouTube that has instrumental music and scripture verses. I turn the lights out and show one to demonstrate how peaceful just five minutes of meditation and music can calm our nature and prepare us for the day.

Prayer

Lord,

In these extremely stressful times with multiple tasks and deadlines in the workplace, we can lose our peace and become agitated, worried, or anxious. Remind us to stop and lean on you. Cause us to say a quick prayer and give the emotion and the challenge to you. Let us remember to put first things first, knowing that everything else will fall into place.

In Jesus' name, Amen.

Can God Come to Work with Me?

Devotion # 13: Time Submits to the Master

". . . being confident of this very thing, that he who has begun a good work in you will complete it until the day of Jesus Christ." (Philippians 1:6)

Did you know that Jesus was never in a hurry, and He never was late? Everywhere He went, time and circumstances submitted to Him.

He always walked with purpose and toward a destination, and He never worried about His arrival time. Even when Martha and Mary thought He was too late to heal Lazarus, He was right on time to raise him from the dead. (John 11:21)

Jesus is Lord of the universe and Lord of time. The Word says that one day is a thousand to the Lord (Psalm 90:4). God told Habakkuk that the vision "though it tarry" will not be one day late (Habakkuk 2:3).

This has a profound impact on my earthly perspective because it means that God can speed things up or slow things down in the spirit realm. No matter what we do, we cannot impact God's timetable. His Word says that He will complete what He began (Philippians 1:5-7).

What does this mean? It means I am to not waste time and continue to move forward; not fear time because "my times are in the Lord's hands" (Psalm 31:15). It also means that the Lord can redeem the time whenever we may make a mistake with God's plan for our life.

In addition to planning, organizing, and keeping a time management system, I can make sure my compass is "pointed north" toward my Creator. I can commit my way to the Lord, and trust that He will direct my steps to the right place and in the right time.

My last major political assignment for the Lord was in Washington, D.C. as President of the *American Parents Association*. The Lord told me in my heart and through others that the assignment would end and I would be coming away for a season for training. I was advised to "not fear" because when it was time for me to go on the frontlines again I would pick things up as if I had not even been away. I was told, "It would be like I had not missed one step in the plan." This is so comforting to know God is in control.

That was in 1991, when I received that message, and I have been in a training ground ever since obtaining experience in corporations, government, and higher education. I have also earned four degrees since that time. I know when the call comes it will only be "one step" into that open door.

Are you waiting for a dream to come to pass? We must trust in God's perfect timing.

Prayer

Help us to trust that you are never late with your promises. Show us how to pray effective prayers while we are waiting. Send encouraging messages through others or your word when we start to get discouraged. Strengthen us that we do not grow weary in waiting and hoping for our dream to be fulfilled.

In Jesus' name, Amen.

Devotion #14: Imagination

"Now faith is the substance of things hoped for, the evidence of things not seen...By faith we understand that the worlds were framed by the Word of God, so that the things which are seen were not made of things which are visible." (Hebrews 11:1-3)

Did you know that imagination is just a thought away from reality? Jesus knew the power of imagination, or He would not have used parables to make a point. Famous inventions begin in the human imagination.

When scientists and inventors use their imaginations to combine two existing perceptions, the result is called a "synthesis." A synthesis combines two or more pre-existing elements resulting in the formation of something new.

Hewlett-Packard has provided consumers with many inventions that were synthesized through human imagination. After the invention of the calculator, engineers invented a calculator that printed paper.

Later, several engineers determined in their imagination that the printing calculator could expand into a "large printing machine" to be used in conjunction with home computers. It was called the HP Desktop Printer. At the time, skeptics said, "no one needs or wants a printer in their home." Yet today, it is a household item.

Synthesis not only applies to inventions and technological advances, it can also work as a spiritual concept: "combining the Word of God with our faith will result in the formation of what is in our imagination."

If you have a dream in your heart – it started in your imagination. If you are not confessing your dream, then you don't believe it is real. You need to talk about it, pursue it, and envision details about it. You need to see yourself with it, meditate on it, and stick with it in order for it to come to pass.

I am not suggesting you just make-up anything in your imagination. I am suggesting that dreams and visions come to us through our imaginations, and we dismiss them as not being real. The dream, inspiration, or heart's desire was more than likely planted as a seed from the Lord, but we dismissed because it seemed foolish or impossible.

Inventors at the 3M Company often have more faith in their imaginations than Christians have in the promises of God. When they get an idea, similar to Edison and the light bulb, they do not give up. They pursue the vision with tests and trials over and over again until it becomes a reality.

The company *3-M* (famous for Scotch Tape and Post-It Notes) has an interesting philosophy for their inventors. They tell their employees: "Conceive, believe, achieve. Persistence— combined with creativity and faith—is still the best formula for long-term success."

Prayer

Lord,

Put a dream in our hearts and imaginations to create something or pursue something that will give us great purpose and financial success. Help us to have the faith to see those things that are not yet immediately before us. Guide us with our dreams and imaginations toward the destiny you have planned for us from the very beginning and equip us to achieve great things for you.

In Jesus' name, Amen.

Devotion #15: On the Tarmac

"Our soul waits for the Lord; He is our help and our shield. For our heart shall rejoice in Him. Because we have trust in His holy name." (Psalm 33:21)

At the San Francisco airport, just before sunrise, I sat in a plane waiting for takeoff on the tarmac (runway) for 40 minutes, waiting for a thunderstorm to pass. We were delayed at the last minute before when the storm suddenly arrived.

I could see the blue lights on the edge of the runway out the window as I wondered if I would make my connection in Dallas.

I began writing in my journal some thoughts I had about my vision to build a leadership center and I heard the inner voice of the Lord say, "You're on the tarmac, Wendy."

I realized that I was very close to take off for what God had been preparing me for - what God has always referred to as my "747" ministry.

I knew a time was coming, perhaps soon, that God would give the signal (from the flight tower) and the ministry would take off not one minute sooner than planned and safe from any danger of a pending storm.

Even though I can see the end of the runway – I certainly cannot see the final destination. I don't even currently have access to the flight plan.

Type A personalities – high achievers – are impatient and don't like tarmac experiences. Yet – because of the pause at the runway – I was able to hear the still small voice of the Lord speaking to my spirit. Out the window, after the storm passed, a rainbow appeared sending God's love and assurance that everything will come to pass on its appointed day.

Waiting is about trusting and I can trust that God is in charge of the plan and it is up to Him to bring it to pass – not me. My job is to put my hope and expectation in God and simply do each day what He requires of me. As Psalm 62: 5 says, "My soul, wait silently for God alone, for my expectation if from Him."

Prayer

Lord,

Many who are reading to this are still waiting for the vision to be fulfilled. I know they are thinking, "I don't think I really heard from the Lord," or "Too much time has passed for that to be part of His plan." Give all of us hope for our future and for the dream you have given us. As Proverbs says, "Hope deferred makes the heart sick, but when it is fulfilled, it is a tree of life (Proverbs 13:12)." We are still excited about that tree of life you have for us Lord and we are fixing our hope on You, not on the timing.

In Jesus' name, Amen.

Devotion #16: More Than We Ask

"For unto Him who is able to exceedingly abundantly do more than we ask or think according to the power that works in us through Jesus Christ Our Lord." (Ephesians 3:20, Amplified)

God is able to do MORE than we ask or think. When He answers prayer – it is beyond our hopes, dreams, and imaginations. Not only will He exceedingly and abundantly help us – He will also work His power THROUGH us because Jesus lives within us.

For many years I misunderstood a picture of my life vision that a pastor/evangelist had spoken to me. I thought the Lord said, "The open-door God has for your ministry is so big it will seem miles wide and high to you but it really is so small in Holy Spirit's eyes, He has to get down on His knees to look through."

Twenty years later I was reading that message in my journal, and you know what it really said? It said, "From the Holy Spirit's point of view, YOU – Wendy – will have to get down on YOUR hands and knees to go through the door because GOD IN YOU IS BIGGER THAN THE DOOR!" Wow!

In other words, God will have me so equipped and prepared that even if the mission may seem overwhelming – in reality, it will *not* be difficult with God on my side. What a wonderful image of God being BIG in us to do our assigned tasks.

Are you praying for a vision, dream, or mission in your life? Let me share with you what God is exceedingly able to do.

- God is exceedingly able to make you debt free.

- God is exceedingly able to provide you with the resources you need.

- God will exceedingly give you wisdom and grace.

- God is able to exceedingly give you all the gifts and talents you need.

- His power within you will exceedingly give you supernatural health and strength no matter what your age.

The creator of the universe is ABLE to complete His plan for your life – beyond what you can ask, think, or imagine.

Do you have an overwhelming project ahead? Write it down and meditate on the promise – God is Able. God is not only able to give you what you need to succeed – He is faithful to His word and He will do it. And remember – He will do it THROUGH YOU.

Prayer

Lord,

Help us to think big. Help us to expect exceedingly great things. Remind us that with God on our side, nothing is impossible.

In Jesus' name, Amen.

Devotion #17: The God of this Place

"And we know that in all things God works for the good of those who love Him, who have been called according to His purpose." (Romans 8:28)

It is human nature for us to want to "move on" when we have been in a desert or wilderness experience. We look for a way out or an opportunity to escape. There is nothing wrong with looking to the future, but my experience has been that God wants us to discover how He can be the Lord of our situation or what I call "the God of this place."

I wanted my children to go to a private Christian school, but instead the Lord assured me that He could be Lord of the public schools, and I discovered God working in that place. When my education ministry took me to Washington, D.C, I discovered how God was Lord of the politics in that city.

When my political national speaking career ended, I got employment in a corporation as a secretary. It made no sense to me. Yet, I discovered God working in corporations and that he had a plan for me in the workplace. God used the business sector to teach me much of what I know now about leadership and management.

It took me three years or crying and complaining to realize it was God's will for me to be in a corporation. I wonder if the first three years of captivity for the Israelites in Babylon were just as confusing. Even though Jeremiah told them to "settle in and get comfortable," there was probably that nagging "complaining spirit" that wished for something better and longed to go home.

What does it mean to "find God in this place" and what practical steps do you take? It means that you have to get closer to God, because without a personal daily relationship, the loneliness, pressure, stress, persecution, and strange culture are too much to endure by yourself.

Another great tip I can share is schedule time to do things that you love while you are waiting for the job you want. If you love animals, go to the zoo. If you love nature, go hiking. If you love socializing, plan a dinner evening with friends. If you love games, plan a game night. Remember, there is joy in the ordinary things of life.

Prayer

Lord,

Thank you that you are with us in every place. That you that you have a perfect plan. Help us to find joy in the ordinary things of life. Remind us to think of others in the workplace rather than thinking only of ourselves.

In Jesus' name, Amen.

Devotion # 18: Character Matters

"But Daniel purposed in his heart that he would not defile himself with the portion of the king's delicacies, nor with the wine which he drank...in all matters of wisdom and understanding about which the king examined [him], he found [him] ten times better than all the magicians and astrologers who were in all his realm." (Daniel 1:8 & 20)

There are many examples of people demonstrating character in the Bible. My favorite is Daniel. Here is a man who advanced from slavery to governor of the land. I believe the promotion was more about his character than his skill. God favored him with wisdom because of his obedience.

Daniel ate the right foods according to his religion, refusing the king's dainties. He was excellent in his behavior. He wasn't afraid to speak the truth, and he put God's Word above the intimidation of the world.

I admire Daniel for facing the pressures of a secular society and refusing to participate in things that God would not approve. In today's politically correct environment, it's much easier to go along with the status quo and not cause conflict.

Daniel's one small step of faith and obedience was actually the preparation for something greater. God had to know that He could trust Daniel for a higher calling. Further down the road, Daniel refused to bow down and worship an idol of the king, and he was thrown into the lion's den. He was untouched by the lions and the king worshipped Daniel's God.

Ignoring character, even in the little things, can prevent us from going to the next level. Time spent in education, networking, and skill-building is important, but it is the time spent in God's Word and obeying His commands is what will bring us new levels of responsibility and advancement.

One of the Godly character traits that Daniel demonstrated was excellence. He taught us by example that there were no shortcuts. From the completion of tasks to the treatment of people, Daniel walked as an example of God's truths. He demonstrated to us the importance of excellence in both our words and deeds.

When we can say "yes" to God and "no" to the things of the world – we will be ready to move to the top, and no pressure will cause us to worship the idol of what other people think.

I personally believe that it is when we are under pressure, we can make character mistakes. When our job, dignity, or reputation is at stake, we are tempted to be defensive, compromise, or perhaps tell a small lie to protect ourselves from adverse circumstances.

When someone is rude to us, we are tempted to snap back. When we are late and disorganized, we are tempted to be in a hurry and cause mistakes. These are character shortcuts that can take us away from the peace of God and impact our personal success.

The best thing you can do is be aware and be present. When a personality or situation starts swirling around you, raising your emotions, and you feel pride rising to the surface – stop! Recognize what is happening and immediately focus and go into slow motion. Pull back, take a deep breath, slow down, say a little prayer, recognize the enemy's strategy, and refuse to compromise. Don't eat the king's dainties.

Prayer

Lord,

Let an excellent spirit be upon us as it was on Daniel. Holy Spirit, guide us to make right character decisions in those high-pressure moments. Use us to be an example of strength, light and leadership in this corrupt world. Work through us and advance us where we can have the most influence.

In Jesus' name, Amen.

Devotion #19: Being Stretched

"I will sing of mercy and justice; to you, O Lord, I will sing praises. I will behave wisely in a perfect way, oh, when will You come to me? I will walk within my house with a perfect heart." (Psalm 101:1-2)

In the late 1980s, I was President of the American Parents Association in Washington DC – lobbying for moral values in public school legislation. One evening I felt sorry for myself and I called my husband from a Washington D.C. apartment, crying about a personal minor conflict I had with a former Congressman. I was licking my wounds all alone in my apartment, wanting to be home with my family not in D.C.

I cried and complained to my husband, "Why is this happening to me? I don't deserve this." He calmly replied, "Because God is stretching you and preparing you?" I retorted in a rather unkind way, "Well why isn't He stretching you? Why is it always *me*?" He calmly replied, "Because you are called to a great task and I am not."

I knew he was right. Instead of having a pity party, I needed to accept the stretching. That night I grew up a little.

Remember how I asked my husband, "Why isn't God stretching you?" Well the truth was, my dear husband was being stretched with job, home, and family responsibilities without me being there, but he didn't complain. He knew we were in the calling together.

Prayer

Lord,

Thank you for understanding our emotions and being patient with us. Help us to realize that stretching is good for us and builds character and faith. In those times we are frustrated or lonely, encourage and refresh us. I know you want the best for us and that does not necessarily mean the easiest for us. We trust your plan and your process.

In Jesus' name, Amen.

Devotion #20: Suddenly

"[Watch] lest He come suddenly and unexpectedly and find you asleep" (Mark 13:36, Amplified)

I love it when things happen suddenly. Just when you think you can't wait any longer – God shows up on the scene. Just when you think you are too weary – He gives you a second wind. Just when you think you can't pray one more prayer – your prayer gets answered.

The Lord is encouraging me to tell my listeners that all of you are going to have a suddenly very soon. There is breakthrough coming, and when the windows of Heaven open up – thousands of answered prayers are going to explode on the earth.

I can hear an explosion in the spirit realm – an explosion of God's goodness. The world in general may experience economic distress and earthquakes – but God's people are going to experience an explosion of His favor.

In my executive sales position, I would travel to many conferences and take clients out to dinner. Sometimes I got the fun experience of discovering a brother- or sister-in-the-Lord – other times it was strictly business.

On one occasion, I met a new sister-in-Jesus. She said in a Southern "twang" – "Honey, if you want to know about how God does things suddenly – let me tell you a story. One day I was a college administrator, happy with my life, and in literally a split second, I was a pastor's wife!"

She explained how her and her husband were enjoying their careers and preparing for an excellent retirement with benefits. Suddenly, with no warning, their pastor decided to retire, called her husband in, and said that the Lord told him to appoint her husband to replace him if the board would approve.

She wasn't worried and didn't believe it would ever happen. It was a prestigious African American Church, and there were several pastors who put in their time in the community who would jump at the opportunity. She basically said, "Yeah right – that's not going to happen."

That next Sunday morning, the pastor announced his retirement, a board member put forward a vote of confidence, the board voted, the membership said "aye" and in a split second without an interview or a job posting – her husband was the pastor. He must have been the right man, because he grew the church from 180 to 3,000 members!

It was the most challenging experience of her life time. In fact, when he was appointed, she ran out of the church – overwhelmed – saying to God, "But you didn't ask *me*! I don't want to be a pastor's wife." But God has been faithful and equipped both of them for their new adventure.

My point is – something is just around the corner and God wants to ask, "Are you alert? Are you ready? Are you prepared?" Don't let the suddenly catch you asleep.

Prayer

Lord,

Some of us are ready for a suddenly and others prefer the status quo. Open our hearts to be prepared for what You want. Thank you for equipping and preparing us for whatever lies ahead. We are ready to serve.

In Jesus' name, Amen.

Devotion #21: Under New Management

"For this reason we also, since the day we heard it, do not cease to pray for you, and to ask that you may be filled with the knowledge of His will in all wisdom and spiritual understanding; that you may walk worthy of the Lord, fully pleasing Him, being fruitful in every good work and increasing in the knowledge of God; strengthened with all might, according to His glorious power, for all patience and longsuffering with joy; giving thanks to the Father who has qualified us to be partakers of the inheritance of the saints in the light." (Colossians 1:9-12, New King James Version)

If Jesus was your manager, how would you perform? The truth is - Jesus *is* your boss. When you made Him Lord of your life, you came under new management. Every concept you had about what was right and true is now yielded and submitted to Him.

"Yielding" or "submitting" to someone else's direction for our lives is a difficult concept in this modern age. Since the 1960's – Baby Boomers and their children have been raised in a philosophy of "my rights" and "my freedoms."

It's hard to understand what Apostle Paul meant when he said, "I am now a slave to Christ." It means – no longer my will – but God's will.

The sooner we understand we are under new management and yield to it, the faster we grow closer to the purposes of God, and the more content we become.

I grade papers for Crossroads Bible Institute – a Bible correspondence course for prisoners. I was impressed with a message in one of their lesson plans:

> "If there is no change in our hearts when we are saved, if there is no true desire to begin our lives under new management, if we do not acknowledge that Jesus is now our Lord and Master, then we will have to seriously question whether we have ever truly been saved in the first place." (Crossroads Roadmap #7)

Perhaps you are called to leadership or you have what the Western world calls an "entrepreneurial spirit." Whether you're just starting out, or whether you've been in management for many years, it's good to be reminded that no one starts out on top. Even the greatest of leaders has to start out reporting to other managers. God uses these experiences to prepare us.

God's "new management" of our lives means we must find out the vision of Jesus, our boss, and discover the direction He wants us to go. His directions are found in the Word of God and are taught by the Holy Spirit as we pray. In every area of our lives, including the workplace, God is our personal life coach and mentor, moving us to a higher performance.

In the secular world, there is a practical term called, "managing up." Instead of wishing your boss understood you, you rather work to understand your boss and determine his or her priorities. Once you know the priorities of your boss, you incorporate those in your daily tasks. Some of the most successful leaders are ones that learned to manage up.

Prayer

Lord,

Teach us what your priorities are so that we can make them our priorities. Help us to yield and submit to your ways. Cause us to make your vision for our lives a priority.

In Jesus' name, Amen.

Devotion #22: God's Glory – Not Ours

"And whoever exalts himself will be humbled, and he who humbles himself will be exalted" (Matthew 23:12)

I was watching a talent show on national television with my daughter. One of the participants, a male singer, was very good. He was starting late in life with his dream to sing, and this show was his opportunity.

My daughter told me that he was eliminated in the first round (based on a viewer voting system). Then one of the finalists had an injury and dropped out. The show re-tabulated the results of eight eliminated contestants, and this male singer made it back into the competition.

On his next performance he surprised the judges with an extraordinary performance. As I watched, knowing his story, something in my spirit said, "He's a Christian and he has given this to God." At the end of his performance, the judges pushed him for an answer to describe how he was feeling about his unusual circumstances – first being out – now being in and on his way to one of the top ten performances.

His humble response: "It must be God's will for me to be here."

I said to my daughter with excitement, "I thought he was a believer! I could see the light in his eyes. But why did it have to be so hard for him? Why couldn't he just have gotten in the first time? Why did the others have it so easy? It's always a battle – always a battle for the believers."

My daughter immediately replied, "Because if it was easy, he would get the glory, but when it is impossible, God gets the glory. Everyone now has to admit God's hand was upon him." Why didn't I say that! She was absolutely right – millions of people were watching and God received the glory.

John Maxwell, executive coach and leadership author, writes: "All leaders experience both good and bad days. The key question on your bad day is: Are you going to give up or get up? And how can you get up?"

I think we get inspired to build something - to pursue our dream - and then the enemy attacks. In a state of confusion - we stop. It then takes more energy to "push" toward the goal from that stopped position of discouragement.

If we keep moving in a momentum of faith and not allow ourselves to be defeated, we will have victory and see the vision fulfilled. Sadly, many of us give up at the half-way point just before the victory. We need to encourage each other to complete the race and rebuke the devourer of our hopes and dreams who Jesus calls a liar.

If you are applying for jobs - keep applying. If you are working to get out of debt - keep making payments no matter how small. If you are standing on God's promises for a healing - keep quoting the healing scriptures. If you are trying to turn a company around - keep pursuing your goals. Give God something to work with - keep something in motion for His hand to touch and a powerful force of victory will be the result.

Prayer

Lord,

I sense that your children are weary and tired of standing in faith for Your promises. The waiting can be hard on the flesh and stretch our faith to its limits. Help us to keep the momentum and to keep putting one foot in front of the other, trusting that you put us on this path and what you began, You alone will finish.

In Jesus name, Amen.

Devotion #23: Showroom Christians

"Not that I have now attained this, or have already been made perfect, but I press on to lay hold of and make my own, that for which Christ Jesus has laid hold of me and made me His own." (Philippians 3:12)

After many years of trying to be a "good Christian," I finally figured out that Wendy could not do it, and I had to let Jesus be a Christian through me. God does not want perfect Christians to put in a showroom for all to see. Instead, the only perfection we should be working on is our perfection with our relationship with Jesus.

There was one point in my life that I was broken and ashamed of my failure as a Christian. I was completely empty inside and felt like I would never have anything to give God again. In fact, I could not even imagine why He would even want to use me.

An evangelist looked at me one day in a prayer meeting and said, "Your vessel is completely drained out and empty, isn't it?" I said with tears in my eyes, "Yes."

"Good!" he exclaimed! "Now God can finally pour Himself in you and use you!"

Over the next four years, I won a school board election, wrote a book on school boards, and traveled to 44 states giving school board training workshops.

An organization evolved called The American Parents Association. Its member's lobbied schools and legislatures for local control, parent rights, and morally sound curriculum. It is estimated that at least 2000 Christians or political conservatives won their school board elections as a result of a four-year ministry.

I tell you this story to encourage you that when you feel the weakest, suddenly God will be His strongest. All this success happened because I let God pour himself through me to do His will, even though I did not feel worthy of the task.

If we dwell in Him, His characteristics will begin to pour out of us, and others will be drawn to HIM because of this relationship – not because of our so-called perfect Christianity. In fact, it is Christians judging others in the Christian showroom that is driving people away from God today.

People are hungry for something real, relevant, and loving in their lives and only Jesus can provide that.

Prayer

My prayer is to not be "full of myself" but to be full of God. Remind me Lord to let go of every self-centered thought that either thinks "I can do it" or fears "I can't do it" and rely on You and what you want to do through me. Help me to be real, relevant, and loving to others in my daily job assignments.

In Jesus name, Amen.

Devotion #24: The Path to God's Heart

"Whatever you did for one of the least of these – you did for me"
(Matthew 25:40)

Do you realize it is very easy to please God? Some of us may think it is necessary to complete a long list of accomplishments in order to reach His heart – but God sent His Son to tell us a simple message - "Love God and love our neighbor" (Luke 10:27). Jesus teaches his disciples to reach out to those in despair, poverty, loneliness, or hopelessness.

When my husband worked in Portland, Oregon, he would often go for walks on his lunch break along the Willamette River. One day he heard the Lord speak to him gently in his heart. That evening, he told me with excitement, "I heard the Lord tell me that He is pleased with us."

I couldn't wait to discover why God was so proud of us. I asked, "What did He say? What pleases Him?" He replied, "He thanked us for caring about the least of His." I replied, "I don't understand."

My husband explained how pleased the Lord was that we had let three homeless women on three different occasions live in our home; how we had shared our home and limited resources with foreign exchange students so they could experience America; and how we cared for hurt and abandoned animals.

Finally, the Lord was pleased at how we welcomed the neighborhood children into our home sharing time and love. In my youth and amazement, I asked, "That's it? That's what impresses the Lord?"

I sat in wonderment at how simple it really was to please God. My husband and I refer to those days as our "season of poverty." But now I realize how rich we really were.

The greatest struggle many of us have today with giving, serving, and charity is lack of time or resources. We are convinced that our schedules are so extremely busy and our finances so tight that we don't have time or money for anyone but our jobs and our families.

I am of the theory that when we give of our time and resources, *we gain time and resources.* The investment will never rob us – it will increase us both on earth and in heaven. It's called seed planting and harvest.

I am sure you have heard the expression, "First Things First." Make a list of some charities, missions, homeless shelters, prisons, schools, churches, or animal shelters you would like to support.

Determine in your heart if you would like to give time, food, clothing, or money – and then do it. Consider organizing a charitable event with your work team. Plan a service day with your company. Teach others the joy of giving. You will be glad you did and it will please the Father.

Prayer

Lord,

I'm sorry if I haven't been tuned in to the needs of others. Speak to my heart about where Your Love is needed, and I will pursue giving unto others. I know if I do it unto the least of yours I do it unto Jesus. Direct my steps and my giving,

In Jesus' name, Amen.

Devotion #25: Stand in the Gap

"I sought for a man among them who would make a wall and stand in the gap before Me on behalf of the land, but I found no one" (Ezekiel 22:30)

In September 2008, *Hurricane Ike* was heading our way in central Texas. The storm was 600 miles wide. It was predicted that the Island of Galveston would be wiped off the map, and the city of Galveston on the mainland would be mostly destroyed.

My husband and I were glued to the television to hear the reports and see the direction the storm would take. The mayor of Galveston called for a mass evacuation, and the people were told "to stay would be certain death." Police officials were telling those who refused to leave to write their social security number on their arm, so that their bodies could be identified.

Just before the storm hit shore, the news media was filming the 15-foot waves hitting the levy wall next to Galveston city. The levy wall was only 17-feet high, and waves were predicted to reach 20-feet.

One of the last reporters remaining on the levy in front of a camera was explaining the seriousness of the storm when the camera moved to the right to show a mother with two little girls standing there looking at the Gulf of Mexico. The reporter, barely able to stand against the force of the wind, was shocked. He asked the mother, "What are you doing here?"

She replied, "My girls have never seen the waves like this – it's a once in a lifetime event for them." You could tell by the look on the reporter's face he was thinking, "It's going to be their last event!" The newscaster, being careful not to frighten the little girls, asked if she knew about the evacuation and about the message of the social security numbers. (He was careful not to mention "certain death" in front of the girls).

The woman replied that she heard the warning, but she didn't want to leave her home. She continued, "If I leave and it is all destroyed, what will I do? I need to stay and try to protect it the best I can." The newscaster tried one more time, "You won't be able to save your house – but you can try to save something more important, your children."

Her final word: "I guess us "Galvestonians" are just stubborn; what can I say?" I reacted with anger and yelled at the TV screen, "How stupid can you be? – *you* can choose to kill yourself – but you have no right to take your children with you!"

The storm was predicted to hit Galveston at 2:00 AM. At exactly that time, the Lord woke me. I heard the words "stand in the gap," and I had a visual of those little girls. I began to pray for their safety and protection and continued to pray for the people of Galveston.

That morning I began to think about those words, "stand in the gap." My anger toward someone's ignorance and rebellion turned into mercy. If the woman was standing alone on the shore, everyone watching would say, "She deserves to die." But our second response upon seeing the children would be, "The children don't deserve to die." God's response was, "I am a merciful God, and I want them *all* to live."

I realized that God wants us to stand in the gap on behalf of those that are behaving in unloving, immoral, and destructive ways, and He wants us to pray for mercy until the revelation of Jesus Christ comes to them.

This is something Christian workers can do for stressful and challenging work places – they can stand in the gap. God wants the best for your boss, and the employees. Stand in the gap with prayer.

Prayer

Lord,

I lift up the leaders and employees in my workplace. Give me a heart of compassion for their situations, especially if they don't know you. Let your love shine through me to others and let me be a messenger of hope. I stand in the gap for my company and ask you to bless and prosper it so that people can provide for their families. I pray that the goods and services will benefit mankind.

In Jesus' name, Amen.

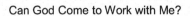

Devotion #26: The Premier Mindset

"For I say, through the grace given unto me, to every man that is among you, not to think of himself more highly than he ought to think; but to think soberly, according as God has dealt to every man the measure of faith." (Romans 12:3)

I heard a keynote speaker from Gaylord Hotels give a presentation on "STAR" customer service. The concept was, "Every customer is a Star and should be treated as one." The keynote speaker shared a lesson from a Nashville comedian Minnie Pearl who had this philosphy: "Perform with the same passion and professionalism for every audience, large or small, because you never know who you are presenting to."

Minnie had missed an opportunity with an agent when she was young because she only gave a minimal performance to a small audience instead of giving her best. The agent refused to hire someone that lacked passion for every person.

When I was a Premier with United Airlines – I was treated like royalty. I was given upgrades to First Class and if a plane was delayed, I was scheduled on another flight immediately. It was awesome!

Years later, I flew United again, but not with the Premier status. I was in the back of the plane with 40 teenagers returning from Washington D.C. to Los Angeles. The flight took an additional hour because of storms – increasing my flight time from five to six hours! How I longed to be in First Class.

When I got to Los Angeles at 10:30 PM, I missed the last flight to Palm Springs. I was directed by security to go downstairs to United. I went up to a counter with three employees and no customers. I tried to get assistance, exhausted from a turbulent and noisy flight, but I was told with all three staring at me, "We can't assist you because this is the Premier Desk." I was in disbelief and protested, "Certainly you can give me some information." I was instructed to go to the next terminal for the "Non-Premier" people.

When I got to the next terminal, I was greeted by a smiling person who went out of her way to help me and treat me with respect. She didn't even know I had over 400,000 miles with United. I asked for her business card and let United know how she saved the day and saved my attitude toward United. I got home by shuttle at 2AM, but I wasn't emotionally distressed, because one person made me feel like royalty even though I was "not a Star" in their system.

I believe Jesus wanted to remind me that every person is *Premier* in His Kingdom and to treat everyone with equal love and respect.

Prayer

Lord,

Your word says to not think of yourself better than others. You demonstrated servant love when you washed the feet of your disciples. You taught that the teacher must become the student. Equip me and humble me to be this type of leader and fill me with Your fairness and justice. Let me see others through your eyes.

In Jesus' name, Amen.

Can God Come to Work with Me?

Devotion #27: Great Expectations

"I pray also that the eyes of your heart may be enlightened in order that you may know the hope to which He has called you, the riches of his glorious inheritance in the saints, and His incomparably great power for us who believe." (Ephesians 1:18)

I had a dream that I was just about to be selected the winner out of three finalists to win a million dollars. I had worked my way through a game show process and now I was in the final three! I had an object in my hand and all the game host had to do was draw the same object out of the bag to match mine and I was the winner!

It seemed to take forever for the drawing to take place. I already knew that I had won. Everything in my spirit told me it was already mine. My prosperity was just a moment away and I was already thinking about what I would tell the watching audience.

When I awoke, I realized what it felt like to expect something with confidence that it was actually going to happen. Later, when I talked to a friend, she and I agreed that we needed to apply this expectation to our future and the promises and vision that God gave us. We needed God's perspective about our future – not the world's perspective.

How does God see our future? He sees us walking in His favor (Deuteronomy 28:2). He sees us running the race and not being moved or turning back (Philippians 2:13). And He sees our purpose and vision arriving right on time – not one day late (Habbakuk2:3).

This week in prayer, I was trying to get the heart of what people were going through and I asked out loud, "I wonder what people on their way to work are thinking about right now?" I heard in my spirit, "They are thinking, 'I wonder if this will ever end? I wonder if this pandemic will ever be over? I wonder if I will ever afford retirement? I wonder if my dream will ever come to pass?'"

Habakkuk asked God the same thing: "How long will I cry for help and You will not hear? (Habakkuk 1:2)" Not all of us are waiting for a big dream, but for those that have a dream that has not yet come to pass, the Lord would say, "I'm working on it – stay with the program – big things take time, so don't get discouraged."

The waiting season has a purpose – it builds strength and character. But we also have to do our part during the waiting – we have to pursue faith and pursue the Word of God. God tells His people through Habakkuk: "Write My Words on your heart and imprint them on your mind."

Waiting for God to change circumstances in the workplace is tough. What can you do to turn things around and bring hope back into your heart during the waiting? Here are some practical ideas that have worked for me:

1. Stop speaking negative thoughts immediately after receiving negative news. Instead, be quiet and be still before the Lord and get His perspective and direction.

2. Find at least three promises about the future plans God has for you and post them where you can view them every day. Focus on His promises – not on the current circumstances.

3. If you are believing for the "perfect" job that allows you to use your gifts and talents, write your dream job down. Meditate on it. Talk about it. Believe for it. (And sign up for job announcements on job search engines.)

4. God works through a spirit of thankfulness so renew your commitment to praise Him in all circumstances.

Waiting for the dream or the promise to be fulfilled is not easy, but you can trust God's character. He knows what we can handle and exactly when we are ready to handle it. Waiting does not mean to stop believing. It means to "wait in faith."

Prayer

Lord,

Help us to continue to wait in faith for your promises. Let us trust that you will not be one day late. Remind us that timing is everything and You have a perfect plan. If I start to get discouraged, bring someone along that will give me words of encouragement. Encourage people right now through this message to not give up. Breakthrough is just around the corner. Thank you for your faithfulness in our lives. Help us be faithful and continue to trust.

In Jesus' name, Amen.

Devotion #28: The Extra Mile – Traffic Free

"Let patience have her perfect work, that ye may be perfect and entire, wanting nothing." (James 1:4 KJV)

The book of James instructs us to consider it joyful when we encounter trials of any sort. Why? Because "the trial and proving of your faith bring out endurance and steadfastness and patience" (v. 3).

Without trials, we will never be fully developed. When we fail countless times, we see it as failure, but God sees it as marathon training.

We are learning how to walk; He picks us up when we fall down; eventually we are running; and someday we are marathon material. God is a patient God, and He is asking us to allow His patient work to take place in our lives.

James took over the leadership of the Jerusalem church after Peter left Palestine. He presided at the Jerusalem council, where the church leaders, former Jews, reached an agreement for the basis of Christian fellowship.

This man of God has my attention – he is a respected church leader and a great meeting facilitator. I decided to study him further as a leadership example. James was not only concerned with spiritual growth, he was also concerned with the practical and ethical life of Christians.

He believed that a genuine faith must produce good works, or what I call a spirit of excellence. He was very familiar with Jesus' teachings, he was present on the Day of Pentecost, and he sought to preserve the *Sermon on the Mount,* where Jesus spoke to over 10,000 men, women, and children.

James did not like religious hypocrisy. He had an irritation with Christians who would tell a poor person "I'll pray for you" instead of giving him food and clothing.

James was unwavering in his faith, and he tells us, if you want wisdom, then ask for it. Obviously, he had firsthand experience with this concept.

James is a short, but a powerful book on principled and practical Christianity and leadership. James would have liked the leadership teachings of famous Zig Ziglar. Zig would say, "There's no traffic jam on the extra mile."

Leadership author John C. Maxwell comments along these same lines: "If you always do more than is expected, not only will you rise up above the crowd, but you will also help others to rise up with you."

Apostle James, Ziglar, and Maxwell, are telling us to be good Christian examples, and that in the workplace and in leadership, we need to give our all as unto the Lord.

Prayer

Lord, our desire is to serve you with excellence in the workplace so we can be examples of the teachings of Jesus Christ. It's not enough to talk about our faith, but we must be examples of good works and disciplined behavior. It's tempting to just get by with average performance; help us to overcome that temptation and run this race to the best of our ability.

In Jesus' name, Amen.

Devotion #29: Faithful in the Small Things

For this very reason, adding your diligence (to the divine promises),
employ every effort in exercising your faith to develop virtue
(excellence, resolution, Christian energy), and in (exercising) virtue
(develop) knowledge. (2 Peter 1:5, Amplified)

Peter offers one of my favorite lessons in the Bible, because the theme is knowledge. The words "know" and "knowledge" occur more than sixteen times in this epistle, and there is a focus on character building and the development of "the divine nature" in our daily lives.

Peter tells us in verse five that if we employ every effort to develop virtue (excellence) that in turn we will develop knowledge and intelligence. In verse six, he goes on to say, if we exercise knowledge and develop self-control, steadfastness, and endurance, that in turn we will develop godliness. And in verse seven, if we exercise godliness and develop brotherly affection, that in turn we will develop our ultimate goal – Christian love.

Peter concludes in verse eight, "if we work at having these qualities abound in us, they will keep us from being idle or unfruitful." In other words, if we are not focused on building our character, we become lazy and disobedient. I love the step-by-step growth plan in these four verses. And it all starts with excellence!

Work ethic for God, for our families, or for our workplace begins in our hearts. I call it "a spirit of excellence." James says if we want wisdom, ask for it. I'm pretty sure we can ask for a spirit of excellence too and God will be faithful to provide opportunity for us to grow.

But first, we need to desire to serve God with excellence in small things to achieve excellence in big things. The Bible says about Daniel that there was "a spirit of excellence upon him."

Through obedience, Daniel took steps to serve God in the small things, and later God honored him with large responsibilities. Peter said we should "give all diligence" on forming godly habits. The grace of God that gives us miracles in times of great challenges is the same grace that builds character through our common everyday tasks.

Daniel's life was not only God-given dreams and visions and the lion's den experience. As governor of the land, he faced the daily tasks of paper pushing, project management, government red tape, jealous co-workers, and people conflicts. He prayed on his knees at least three times a day to honor God and to receive from Him grace and strength, character building, wisdom, and direction.

There are no shortcuts to leadership success. Whatever assignments God gives you, do it with excellence. If you are faithful in the small things, He will give you more.

Prayer

Lord,

Help us to be faithful and obedient in the small things and trust that when it is time you will promote us to the bigger assignments and, like Daniel, you will give us the grace and strength to succeed.

In Jesus' name, Amen.

Devotion #30: Maximum Capacity

"Stay here and keep watch with Me." (Matthew 26:38, NLT)

Are you serving Jesus with your maximum capacity? Or do you fall asleep when you enter into prayer or spiritual warfare, because of your own natural limitations? Do you seek help from God first, or as a last resort?

In the Garden of Gethsemane, where Jesus prayed before he was crucified, the disciples fell asleep instead of praying with Jesus. A short time later, when He was arrested, they all fled. After the ascension of Jesus, these former fearful men transformed into bold witnesses for the kingdom of God.

What changed in their lives? Jesus told them, "You will receive power when the Holy Spirit comes upon you …" (Acts 1:8, NASB). Then in Acts 2:4, "They were all filled with the Holy Spirit" (KJV).

To serve Jesus at our maximum capacity, we must listen to the Holy Spirit and be open to His wisdom and teaching. God also desires that we be at our maximum capacity in the workplace or He would not have pointed out to us that Daniel "was excellent in all he did."

A national bestselling secular business book, *Good to Great*, by Jim Collins, offers some research results. Collins confirms that getting the "right" people on board with a project or company is the key to success. Trying to train the "wrong people" is doomed to failure.

Who are the right people? Collins concludes it is disciplined people who apply disciplined thought and action.

What else did Collins discover about great companies? The great companies he studied faced the same world-wide economic crisis as others but survived. Research found a commonality. The CEO's embraced an unwavering faith that they can and will prevail in the end, regardless of the difficulties, and at the same time have the discipline to confront the most brutal facts of current reality.

The most astounding commonality was, the CEO's had gone through their own personal trials and challenges and were not afraid to face the crisis.

Why do you think secular kings promoted Joseph, Nehemiah, Esther, and Daniel into high positions of authority? They were disciplined, gave maximum capacity to their organizations or personal mission, they had faith to prevail, and they depended on prayer to guide them in their decision-making.

Collins asks the question, "What creates enduring great organizations?" His research concludes, "enduring great people."

Excellence means both using all the skills and talents the Lord gives us to the best of our ability and depending on Him completely. In order to live disciplined lives for God and for our organizations, we need to let God have control.

In the book, *God is My CEO,* author Larry Julian notes that the most important relationship the successful CEO's had was the private, ongoing, daily relationship with the Lord. The first step in each CEO's decision was to seek God's wisdom and team-up with the Holy Spirit to get the job done.

Prayer

Lord,

It's hard to imagine having the resolve and leadership skills of a great CEO. My desire is to move from good to great in my own work sphere and responsibilities. I know with the Holy Spirit guiding me, I can do all things you want me to do through Christ who strengthens me. Thank you, Holy Spirit, for guiding me in Your wisdom today.

In Jesus name, Amen.

Devotion #31: Even in the Small Things

"Do all things without grumbling and faultfinding and complaining (against God) and questioning and doubting (among yourselves)." (Philippians 2:14)

On our 35th wedding anniversary (2004), my husband and I went to Gettysburg, Pennsylvania. While in Gettysburg, I visited with the Christian owner, who was 54 and, in a wheelchair, of the bed-and-breakfast where we stayed.

At age 52, she had a sudden brain infection, and it paralyzed the entire left side of her body. She went from actively operating a business to dependence on her husband to do everything.

I asked her if she had learned anything through her circumstances that she could share with me. She said, "People complain too much."

She went on to explain that her church had planned for a different person each week to pick her up and drive her to church. In her paralyzed state and limited speech, she was "locked" in the car with them and forced to listen.

She said, "People whine and complain about the smallest things. For example, they complain about how they are getting old, they share all their little petty aches and pains, as if somehow they were supposed to escape that stage of their life!" She continued, "people need to express more gratitude."

Here is a woman whose life as she once knew it had ended. Her lesson to us is, "be more grateful." She also added, "I pray more. I can't do much of anything else, so I spend most of my day praying for others."

Most of us find it easy to keep the Lord's commandments in the big things. We do not cheat, lie, or steal. It is in the little things that we forget what He requires of us. Jesus said, "If anyone desires to come after Me, let him deny himself . . ." (Luke 9:23, NKJV).

How about the "small" instructions that Jesus gave us to quit worrying about what we wear or what we will eat. Paul wrote to the Philippians, "(Be) content with (your) earthly lot of whatever sort that is, (and that peace) which transcends all understanding shall garrison and mount guard over your hearts and MINDS in Christ Jesus." (Philippians 4:7)

Paul then writes to only think on "whatever is true... noble... right... pure... lovely... admirable... excellent... worthy of praise." (Philippians 4:8, NIV)

The Israelites got stuck in the wilderness for 40 years, because of a very small thing – whining and complaining. I still need to be reminded that God will flow through our praises and our positive attitude – He cannot flow through negativity.

Prayer

Lord,

Thank you for the reminder that you dwell in our praise and thanksgiving. Forgive us our grumbling and complaining. Holy Spirit, help us to do better and fill us with the joy of the Lord.

In Jesus' name, Amen.

Devotion #32: A Covenant Relationship

"I have set my rainbow in the clouds, and it will be the sign of a covenant between Me and the earth." (Genesis 9:13)

The first time I ever heard the word "covenant" was very early in my marriage and about two years after my husband Terry and I accepted the Lord Jesus Christ (almost 50 years ago). We were going through a very difficult time emotionally and financially. In fact, it was so serious, we did not know if the marriage would make it.

We got down on our knees for the first time as a couple to pray to the Lord for His blessing and guidance. My husband said, "I heard the word 'covenant' – the Lord is making a covenant with us to keep us together." We had never heard that word before, so we looked it up.

"Covenant" in *Webster's Dictionary* means "a formal, solemn, and binding agreement; a written agreement or promise under seal between two or more parties for the performance of some action; to enter into a contract." We had such peace in that moment that we knew no matter what the circumstances, God was not only going to work on our behalf, He was also going to prevent the enemy from destroying our marriage.

The covenant will not work unless we participate in our part of the agreement. Many covenant promises in the Bible begin with, "If you only believe…" Our part of the covenant was to believe God's promise for our marriage.

I could list over 100 trials and heartaches that our marriage endured over the past 50 years since we received that message, but we maintained our faith by holding to His promise in each and every situation, and God kept His covenant with us. We learned that Faith believes in the promises of God, not in what we were feeling in each challenge.

Recently, we just faced another challenge and God was faithful to his Word. My husband had a heart attack in the middle of the night. I awoke to finding him close to death. After calling 911, I laid hands on his chest and shouted multiple times, "Jesus help Terry! – Jesus help Terry!" He came back to me and the paramedics arrived to give him a defibrillator shock. The paramedic's said he should not have survived; the doctors were amazed that his heart was not damaged.

I was able to share with my students the power of the name of Jesus. The Lord decided it wasn't time for Terry and His covenant continues in our marriage. The year I am publishing this book, we will celebrate 53 years of marriage. I would like to pray a prayer of gratitude.

Prayer

Lord,

Thank you for your faithfulness to answer prayer. Thank you for the power in the name of Jesus. Thank you for keeping a covenant of love with all of us. Thank you for giving me the faith and strength to get through another challenge. Continue to bless the marriages of all those reading today. Your care for us is amazing.

In Jesus Name, Amen.

Devotion #33: Take it in the Mask

"For me, to live is Christ – His life in me; and to die is gain."
(Philippians 1:21)

What did Jesus mean when He said we must lay down our life to gain our life? It means we need to be accountable to Him for our actions. He meant we must give up our personal rights, give up what *we* want to do, and live for Him.

Giving up your right to hate someone, giving up your right to a job position that someone else received, giving up your right to your finances, or giving up your right to anger or resentment, are all ways we die to self.

Giving up the things that feel good is not easy – that is why it is called death. When those things do not matter anymore, and only Christ matters, then we will be full of life. What exactly do we gain? A sense of wellbeing, peace, treasures in heaven, blessings on earth, a purpose, the joy of knowing Jesus, and a toughness against the attacks of Satan.

The Israelites were slaves to Egypt and then set free. Similarly, we were slaves to sin and are no more condemned. Those bondages to sin were aging us, depressing us, demoralizing us, and killing us. That is why laying down our life is gain.

The greatest thing about being dead to the world and alive in Christ is that you cannot hurt a dead person! Rejection, criticism, persecution, jealousy, and betrayal cannot hurt you when you have given your life completely to Jesus. The challenges and personality conflicts in the workplace will not upset you as you allow Christ to control your life.

My daughter used to be a baseball referee when she was in college. At her first game, when the ball came across the plate, she turned her head away. The coach of one of the teams came up to her and quietly said, "You need to take it in the mask." She asked, "What?" and he replied, "It hurts a lot less to take it in the mask than to take it on the side of the head. The mask is designed to take it. Don't flinch – just take it."

As we follow Jesus and let go of the world, we grow stronger, and we learn to face the enemy with courage. Every time we turn the other cheek, every time we do not retaliate, every time we refuse to gossip, every time we don't let management upset us, every time we overcome hate with love, we soften our heart to Christ, but gain a stronger mask. Eventually we will point to our mask and yell at the enemy, "Throw me your best shot!"

Prayer

Lord,

Help us to die to self and negative emotions that can destroy our peace, our joy, our health, and our love towards others. As we yield to the Holy Spirit, strengthen our resolve to be more like Christ, not be moved by circumstances, and take it in the mask.

In Jesus' name, Amen.

Devotion #34: Casual Christians

"Where there are envy, strife, and divisions among you, are you not carnal . . .?" (I Corinthians 3:3)

Have you ever heard the phrase "carnal Christian" or "casual Christian"? It means Christians walking according to the flesh instead of according to the Spirit. A Christian that gossips, is jealous, gets easily upset, causes strife, or constantly complains is a carnal Christian.

A Christian who does not bear fruit for Jesus or sits on a fence, is a casual Christian.

Apostle Paul recognized this as a common problem when he wrote messages regarding this to the churches of the Romans, Corinthians, Ephesians, and Galatians. Over 2000 years later, Pastors are still preaching the same message – to let your actions speak louder than your words.

Every Christian has the potential of being carnal or casual, but the question is, do you ignore carnality, make excuses for it, deny it, rationalize it, or do you confess it? Paul said, "Walk in the Spirit, and you shall not fulfill the lust of the flesh." (Galatians 5:15)

We alone cannot make it right – we can only confess it. Adam blamed Eve and Eve blamed the snake – it is our nature to not confess – but with Jesus, it is the only choice.

A friend of mine was a State Highway Patrolman for over 20 years. He told me that most people who are pulled over for speeding or other infractions have excuses for their behavior. He heard many creative stories over the years.

He shared that when someone finally admitted they were wrong and gave no excuse, it was so refreshing to hear the truth, that he often would not give them a ticket. He commented that it amazed him that grown adults still behave as children and will not face honestly the consequences of their actions.

My favorite story that explains God's mercy when we make mistakes or sin is the story of Peter. Peter decided to follow Jesus when he was asked to cast his net to the other side of the boat and his net was full.

Peter said he would follow Christ forever and even die for Him. But when the pressure came down at the arrest of Our Lord, Peter denied Jesus three times. He felt like such a failure, the Bible says he went back to fishing.

He must have figured he was not worthy or capable of following God. After the resurrection, Jesus came to the shore and found him and once again told him to cast his net to the others side, and once again the net was full. God's attitude and hope in Peter had not changed. He then told Peter to be a "fisher of men."

In the end, Peter had great faith and upon that faith "the church was built." It was by confession, mercy, and grace – not by trying or being perfect.

Do you feel off track from what God called you to do? Have you wondered if your purpose in your career is what it's supposed to be? Does your net fill empty? God would say, cast your net again with new expectation and call upon the name of Jesus to fill you up with renewed strength, determination, and purpose.

Prayer

Lord,

Forgive us for being carnal or being too casual and being pulled in to a secular worldview instead of a Biblical worldview. We confess our sins and pray you will help us get back on track. Where we have felt empty and purposeless, fill us back up. As David the Psalmist says, "Create in us a clean heart and renew a right spirit within us. Restore unto us the joy of our Salvation."

In Jesus's name, Amen.

Devotion #35: Fresh or Stale?

"Jesus, answered and said to him, 'Most assuredly, I say to you, unless one is born again, he cannot see the kingdom of God'" (John 3:3)

When we prepare our "to do lists" for the week we could develop the Monday morning "blues" – especially if we just had a great weekend. Can you relate? But whenever my assignments become an effort and not a joy, I know it is time to bow my head before the Father to bring the freshness of the Spirit back into my life.

I often sit in my car in the parking lot of my workplace and pray, "Lord, I need confirmation today in the midst of all these tasks that there is a spiritual reason for me to be here and that this job is part of your plan for my *spiritual* life, not just my physical life." I spend time with Him until I felt His peace and strength.

On one such morning, within that same hour I received a call to meet a client at a local television news station that I had talked to on the phone but never met. On the way to the appointment, the Spirit of the Lord spoke to my heart and said, "I am going to confirm to you that this person is a Christian."

By the end of the appointment, the client asked me if I was a Christian and we spent several minutes encouraging each other with the joy of discovering we were believers. I was especially delighted to know that he was a news anchor. I then added this person to my Marketplace Christians devotions list as a leader I needed to pray for in our community. Our families have been friends ever since.

It was such a simple answer to a big prayer, but I returned to work with the joy of the Lord knowing that His destiny in my life is to encourage believers and leaders in the marketplace.

Bruce Wilkinson was inspired to write the book *Secrets of the Vine* because of staleness in his own life. Once he focused less on what he could do for God and spent more time *with* God, he began to bear fruit in his life.

I have two of his powerful statements written in my journal. The first one is: "Unless your friendship with God becomes your first priority, you will never fulfill your true destiny as a Christian or a leader," and the second: "His purpose is not that you will do more for him but that you will choose to be more with Him."

Jesus said, "I am the vine and you are the branches. He who abides in Me, and I in him, bears much fruit, for without me you can do nothing." (John 15:5)

I close with this scripture: Ephesians 6:10 - "Be strong in the Lord – be empowered through your union with Him; draw your strength from Him – that strength which His boundless might provide."

Prayer

Lord,

Let our jobs be more than tasks, goals, and meetings. Cause us to make connections throughout the week where we can encourage others and where others encourage us. Let there be special moments and divine appointments that give us joy. Thank you, God, for all the exciting spiritual things You are doing for us in the marketplace.

In Jesus' name, Amen.

Devotion #36: God is in Control

"We know that all things work together for good to those who love God . . ." (Romans 8:28)

Jesus knew that the reason he was standing before the governor Pontius Pilate because God decided he would stand before him. In the same hour, Jesus had the opportunity to tell Pilate that he was a king only because God decided he was a king.

On one occasion, I was called in to Human Resources. I was told to stop sending Christian devotions to people at work and to stop praying with people. The strength of the Lord came through me as I firmly, but calmly stated, "My communications regarding faith and God are from my home email early in the morning to other home emails and people volunteered to receive them. I do not write them at work, and I do not send them to work addresses."

I continued to tell HR that I know that legally, I can pray on my lunch and breaks when people ask for prayer, and that trying to stop me would not hold up in any court of law. The accusations caught me by surprise, but God gave me peace immediately and words in that same hour. (Matthew 10:19&20)

Please know, that as a manager, I also recognize the wisdom of being balanced in the working world and to "walk carefully." I had walked in excellence on the job and carefully with my faith-based activities.

I talked to my Christian executive coach about the situation, and she asked an interesting question: "Is it possible to receive the painful circumstance of the unjust accusations you received as a 'gift' from God?" I'm not sure I saw it as a gift, but I did respond: "It did reveal to me that time between my fear or emotionalism and my trust that God is in control is getting shorter and shorter. I was at instant peace in my reaction."

My readers may not ever experience anything this severe, but I want to encourage you to be prepared. As you grow in your faith, you will discover that your reaction to these challenging situations will be amazingly calm and you will be full of wisdom instead of fear, because you have spent time in prayer with Him. You will have this overwhelming knowing that God is in Control.

Prayer

Lord,

I ask that as we study your word and spend time with you, you will prepare us to stand calmly in that hour of crisis and trust you are in control. I also ask that when needed, you will give us the words of wisdom we need to speak in that very same hour. Thank you that you have our back, and you are for us. We trust you only want the best for us and that even sometimes a challenging surprise is actually a gift from you to show us how well we are doing in our trust and faith. We love you, Lord.

In Jesus' name, Amen.

Devotion #37: It's Time

"He who dwells in the secret place of the Most High shall remain stable and fixed under the shadow of the Almighty" (Psalms 91:1)

Since the mid-1990s, the Lord has given me a vision of grapes. I cannot stop thinking about them. I have grape paintings in my living room, grapes on my dining room table, and grapes on my charm bracelet.

Along with the vision came the words, "It's Time." When I looked up references to grapes in the Bible, it always referred to "crushing." Of course, I kept telling myself, "it's time for the harvest," or "it's time to develop the fruits of the Spirit," certainly not crushing!

Now, I realize that the last twenty years have been a time of "crushing" to make me into the wine that God needed to pour out to His children. Without the pruning by the Vinedresser, there will only be leaves, not fruit. Without the crushing, there will only be grapes.

What circumstances did God use to squeeze me? Difficult managers, jobs that did not value my talents, people that didn't love me, the loss of several pets, fear of not having enough money, and being stretched to the max with responsibility and schoolwork. Does this sound familiar?

My calling is leadership. Over and over, I have "crushing" experiences that are forming my management skills. I have a friend who is studying to be a counselor. Over and over again, the Lord gives her opportunity to practice interpersonal and conflict resolution skills. The pressure has a purpose – it's to cause us to pour out a refreshing new drink to others.

There is a great crushing happening in the world and people are facing great pressures with earthquakes, hurricanes, job loss, pandemics, and family deaths. If we face these things in our own life with the grace of God and let Him mold us, we will be able to pour ourselves out to others and give them the love of Jesus Christ in their crushing times.

Don't be caught off guard, keep your candle lit, and be prepared in maturity and strength. Yield to Him in the crushing of the grapes and receive with joy His hand upon your life.

What did King David do in one of the most crushing times of his life? When he almost lost his life to the Philistines who wanted revenge for the death of Goliath, he escaped into a cave and sang these words: "I will bless the Lord at ALL times; His praise shall continually be in my mouth. My life makes its boast in the Lord; let the humble and afflicted hear AND BE GLAD. O magnify the Lord with me, and let us exalt His name together." (Psalms 34:1-3)

Prayer

Lord,

Crushing circumstances to make a new wine to pour out to others is hard. But I know you will not allow more than we can endure, and the word says you discipline those you love. I know you are making us into rivers of life for others and I do desire to be used for the purposes of your kingdom. Continue to surround me in those times of trial and let me feel your peace, your presence, and even your joy.

In Jesus' name, Amen

Devotion #38: Leave Room for God

"For no word from God will ever fail." (Luke 1:37)

Are you a multi-tasker or at least trying to be? You can expect God to show up in surprising ways in the midst of your meetings, your presentations, your preaching, your teaching, or your plans, if you make room for God.

There is no mountain of tasks or resistance in your work life or ministry that God is not big enough to overcome. I continue to be inspired by God's concern over the details of my job. I have seen his hand upon so many assignments and challenges. He is the Master Coordinator of our affairs if we will give him a chance to come into our schedules.

Bruce Wilkinson, in the devotional book *The Prayer of Jabez*, asks, "What overwhelms you today? What is the goal you feel incapable of completing? Draw a small picture or symbol of it in a box. Write its name inside the box too. Then draw a wide circle around your box to represent God. He is greater; He surrounds your challenge. Then pray over your drawing until you accept in your deepest heart that God is bigger than any opportunity or any obstacle."

It reminds me of the words of a song by Michal W. Smith: "You may think that you're surrounded, but you're surrounded by me."

For seven years I managed a major Foreign Policy event where 500 people attended lectures for eight weeks. One year, the Professor who we paid to coordinate and moderate the event suddenly stepped down. With God's presence in my life, I immediately chose not to panic and to commit the entire challenge into the Lord's hands. I even contacted some people to pray for me.

At first, I felt a little ashamed asking for prayer for a work request since it may seem minor to other people. God knew however, it was *major* to me, and He was faithful to respond. I left room for Him to create what the event should look like, and I began to make phone calls and do research on the internet to find presenters for eight current world topics of which I had little to no knowledge.

God gave me favor, and one-by-one people came into my life, supported me, found other contacts, and helped me to be successful. The event was a huge success.

One example of the miracle God did for me was trying to find an expert in Southern California on "Sudan and the War in Darfur" (Africa). My research through government agencies in Los Angeles (the closest big city) and through the Anti-Defamation League, confirmed there was only one expert on this topic.

He was a Crisis Consultant, lived in Washington D.C, and was presently visiting Sudan several times a year. In faith, I contacted him, and he agreed to speak. He arrived in Washington D.C. from Sudan one week before the event, flew to my community to present, and flew back to Africa two days later.

God did not want just anyone – he wanted the best! I stayed within budget during that crisis AND God gave increased revenue for the college of $12,000! He helped me *beyond* my expectations!

Invite God into your projects and leave room for surprises. A famous American clergyman, Phillips Brooks, wrote: "Do not pray for tasks equal to your powers. Pray for powers equal to your tasks."

Prayer

Lord,

Many of my readers have some great tasks before them or challenging projects to manage. May they lean on you and seek your face and know that nothing is too great for you. I love your word that says, "My arm is not too short." We receive your power and direction now into our current or next challenge. Thank you for walking with us on this journey.

In Jesus' name, Amen.

Devotion #39: Let Your Yes be Yes

"Samuel was afraid to tell Eli the vision." (I Samuel 3:15)

Samuel, a youth, heard a message from God and had to tell his elder Eli, a priest in the temple, that Eli was in sin and that the nation was in danger. It is difficult to be obedient to God when you have to give bad news, or you have to say something that makes people uncomfortable.

God is teaching me that good leaders do not hold back or avoid the truth. They speak the truth in love. Samuel had to do what was best for the nation and today managers often have to do what is best for the organization. Tough love may be painful to facilitate or participate in, but other employees will be grateful for your tough leadership choices that in the end benefit everyone.

I asked a successful CEO and millionaire, what one piece of advice would he give me? He said, "Be honest with people. Don't put flowers in front of it and flowers at the end of it. Just speak the truth in kindness and do what you know to be the right thing."

Another leader told me, "God says let your 'yes' be 'yes' and your 'no' be 'no.' There is no in the middle with God." (Matthew 5:31)

The best advice I can share with my readers is that employees and managers appreciate the truth and the best way to give feedback is stick to the facts and limit the emotion. State briefly what concerns you. Give a recent example of what concerns you. Share the impact the concern has on others or the company. And ask the person if they have a solution. If they don't –offer your proposal for a solution. End the conversation with appreciation for being open to discussion and then you need to be willing to accept feedback for your part of the problem.

Brene' Brown, author of Dare to Lead, writes: "Leaders who live into their values are never silent about hard things."

Prayer

Lord,

Give us the courage to be open and honest and deliver tough messages with both directness and kindness. Help us to do what's right for the team and the organization even if it means facing fears and feelings. I want to embrace the ability to give and receive feedback. Holy Spirit give me the wisdom to do it with excellence and humility.

In Jesus' name, Amen.

Devotion #40: May His Force be with You

"Roll your works upon the Lord – commit and trust them wholly to Him; He will cause your thoughts to become agreeable to His will, and so shall your plans be established and succeed." (Proverbs 16:3)

Paul in the Bible describes his calling as a necessity laid upon him. That means no matter what his mind tells him or how his heart tries to discourage him, something in his spirit drives him to be an evangelist until the day he dies.

Some people are afraid of receiving "a call" from God because they think it will be so big, so difficult, or so time consuming, they will not be able to do it. I can attest that it is not like that.

When God drops a call into your spirit to do something, it is like a "force" that drives you and consumes you and you have a *desire* to do it. In fact, you are miserable if you don't do it.

I served as the Faculty Advisor to the Student Christian Club (Campus Crusade for Christ) at a college in California. Each year it was a challenge to get the district to agree to a room location, to provide audiovisual equipment for educational videos, or to coordinate non-work-related activities in my work schedule.

It was God's call, so I let God work it out. Each semester a room would open up and God would give me the time and leaders to help. Through the club, at least two students accepted Jesus as their Savior and each year, dozens of Christian students were encouraged through Biblical teachings.

Toward the end of my service to the club, pastors were volunteering from all over the community from different denominations to meet the students and share a message of faith and the burden was no longer just mine.

Jesus promised that the burden he gives us is light. It becomes light because He gives us the resources and people to carry it out. He does not forsake us.

If you do not feel called to your job or if you do not have a clear sense of God's purpose for your life, begin to pray for that direction. Spend time in prayer, discover what your gifts and talents are (those things you love to do), be open to God using you right where you are, and journal your thoughts and ideas to help you explore what God created you for in this world.

Inside each of us is a "knower" that just knows the right thing to do. Once it is clear in your "knower" that you are called for a certain purpose, task, project, marriage, ministry, or job, REST in knowing that He will help you achieve your goals. May the FORCE OF GOD be with you.

Prayer

Lord,

Stir up within us and make us aware of our unique gifts and talents and then direct our paths to where and how you want us to use them. When we hear our purpose in our "knower," equip us with everything we need to succeed. My heart's desire is to respond in obedience when you call.

In Jesus' name, Amen.

Devotion #41: People are Watching You

"If I be lifted up (from the earth), I will draw all men unto Me." (John 12:32)

How do we lift up the name of Jesus in the workplace? Unfortunately, some believe it means to quote the Bible to a captive audience. This approach will not only get you in trouble, but it has also not been very successful in drawing people to Jesus.

The Supreme Court has ruled that you cannot evangelize someone in the workplace *against his or her will* and losing your job does not give God any glory. It is okay for your co-workers to know you are a Christian, but as you share stories of your weekend or things you care about, they will know you are a Christian because of the Fruits of the Spirit found in Galatians 5:22-23: "love, joy, peace, patience, kindness, goodness, faithfulness, gentleness, and self-control." And the word says about the fruits, "against such things there is no law that can bring a charge."

How do we accomplish all these wonderful interpersonal and integrity fruits or skills in our lives? The answer is spending time with Jesus.

As we spend more time with Him and in His Word, we become more like Him. As we become more like Him, people at work begin to see Jesus in us. People will notice a life controlled by the Holy Spirit and they will be curious about the peace, love, and joy in our lives.

I have had dozens of opportunities to share God's love and example with co-workers, but I have only had three precious incidents in my 30-year career as a leader where a professional said to me, "There is something different about you – what is it that motivates you?" It was in those moments that I actually got to verbally acknowledge my Lord and His power in my life. These moments were always well timed, well received, and part of God's plan.

After many years in one organization, I did not think anyone noticed my faithfulness to be kind and patient in the midst of some tough circumstances. After I departed, one of the coworkers said, "I admired you for the way you behaved when you were treated badly and you left with a class act. You were positive, with a smile on your face, and never said one bad thing about the organization or leadership to anyone. I have so much admiration and respect for what you did."

My behavior opened a door for a closer relationship with this person and eventually I was able to share how my faith was the anchor of my soul in tough storms. (Hebrews 6:19)

Galatians 5:25, concludes: "If we live by the Holy Spirit, let us also walk by the Spirit. If by the Holy Spirit we have our life in God, let us go forward walking in line, our conduct controlled by the Spirit."

People are watching you. Your example and your actions can be the greatest witness for Jesus on the face of the earth – for your co-workers, your children, your friends, your students, and your family.

Prayer

Lord,

We want others to know your love and the gift of your salvation, but it's hard to share in the workplace. Remind me every day that my actions speak louder than words. When the door opens to share your name, give me the courage to step through and tell others about You.

In Jesus' name, Amen.

Devotion #42: Pour from the Overflow

". . . separated to the gospel of God . . ." (Romans 1:1)

The Spirit of the Lord has impressed on my heart to tell others to not pour yourselves out to others (in ministry or in our jobs) to such a degree that the well of our soul becomes dry. But rather pour from "our overflow" – from the abundance of spending time with God.

Paul in the Bible was one of the greatest Christians who ever walked the earth. He endured suffering, he traveled extensively, he was content, he had joy, he was a tent maker and provided for himself, he was the Apostle of the original churches, he wrote numerous letters, he preached, and he spread the gospel wherever he went.

Yet, he rarely spoke of his character, or his accomplishments and he never mentioned weariness.

He always spoke of Jesus, and he regularly mentioned how he separated himself to God. His eyes were not focused on his own personal holiness or tasks – but rather on the mission God had given him and on his relationship with God.

Many Christian churches have failed to be powerful and effective because people focus on their own holiness and the holiness of others rather focusing on their desire to know God. If we were all focused on God, and not on others, there would be an overflow of love, salvation, and healing that would spread throughout the land.

In the marketplace, in our churches, and in our homes, we are being stretched in multiple directions. With increased responsibilities, world stresses, high self-expectations, new technologies, it sometimes seems more than we can endure. Women in particular are balancing home, church, and career in ways that previous generations have not endured.

I am not saying to take on more, and I am not saying there are not some things you need to let go of, but I am saying, if you spend more time with your Creator and His Son, there will be an overflow that you will be able to pour out without draining your spirit and your strength.

Remember what Jesus told the woman at the well – "I will give you living water and you will never be thirsty." (John 4:10)

If you spend time with God, *HE* will let you know what to let go of and what to take on. If He gives you an assignment, He promised that "His burden is light and not heavy (Matthew 11:30)," and you will be able to endure.

I realize now, that when Jesus turned the water into wine, the greater miracle was "it never ran out!" Meditate on these truths from God:

"Let those who love Your Name be joyful in You and be in high spirits." (Psalms 5:11)

"My faith does not rest upon the wisdom of men but in the Power of God!" (I Corinthians 2:5)

"Not by might, not by power, but by my Spirit, says the Lord." (Zechariah 4:6)

Prayer

Lord,

May God bless the work of your hands as you work for Him. May you complete the tasks set before you with His strength, wisdom, and peace overflowing through you.

In Jesus' name, Amen.

Devotion #43: Producing Grapes for Jesus

"I am the vine, you are the branches: He that abides in me, and I in him, the same brings forth much fruit: for without me you can do nothing" (John 15:5)

How do we abide? We need to spend more time with Our Lord in prayer and in His Word. I like to refer to abiding as "Jesus plus nothing." We cannot do anything of ourselves to produce grapes.

Only Jesus can produce the grapes if we plug in to Him – the Vine. However, abiding does take some effort in prayer and reading the Word.

Gloria Copeland of Kenneth Copeland Ministries confirms this when she wrote: "Abiding in Jesus isn't something that comes automatically to any believer. It's a lifestyle that involves discipline and effort. We have to choose to give ourselves to our union with Him, to give Him first place where our attention is concerned. If we want to grow spiritually, if we want to walk in power and in fellowship with the Lord, we'll have to spend the time it takes to know Him."

This seems like a good place to repeat what Bruce Wilkinson, author of *Secrets of the Vine*, said:

1) His purpose is not that you will do more for him but that you will choose to be more WITH him.

2) Unless your friendship with God becomes your FIRST PRIORITY, you will never fulfill your true destiny as a Christian or a leader.

The higher up in responsibilities we attain in the marketplace, the less time we seem to have to abide. Men and women constantly ask me, "How can we possibly do it all?" I tell them it's not about you – it's about the time spent with God.

In addition to our work responsibilities, Jesus also gives us instruction to bear fruit by giving to the poor, expressing the fruits of the Spirit, taking care of our relatives, and sharing the gospel. To produce "much fruit" for God as the Bible instructs, seems impossible. But God said that if He calls us to do it, He will enable us and that the burden will be light.

There is only one possible way to produce these many grapes for God – let Him do it through us. Spend time with Him instead of time trying to figure it out or worrying.

Ephesians 6:10 summed it up best: "Be strong in the Lord – be empowered through YOUR UNION with Him; draw your strength from Him – that strength which His boundless might provides."

Prayer

Lord,

We make a commitment to spend more time with you and to lean on you more. Not because you require it, but because we know it is time well spent and you desire it of us so that you can strengthen us and equip us. Forgive us for being too busy and not putting you first. Help us to remember to seek first the kingdom of God and know that everything else will be added unto us – even the time to get everything done. Thank you, Lord, for working with us on all our tasks and responsibilities.

In Jesus' name, Amen.

Devotion #44: Being Fully Persuaded

"Yet he did not waver through disbelief in the promise of God, but was strengthened in his faith and gave glory to God, being fully persuaded that God was able to do what He had promised. This is why 'it was credited to him as righteousness.'" (Romans 4: 20)

The promise that Abraham would have a son was fulfilled when he was over 90 years old. What a great example of believing even in old age, that the promise will arrive.

Romans 8:38 says "For I am persuaded, that neither death, nor life, nor angels, nor principalities, nor powers, nor things present, nor things to come can separate us from the love of God." We can firmly believe that God will take care of us in all circumstances.

I learned that we go through stages of faith from belief to knowledge to persuasion to commitment. There are people at each of these levels that will lift us up to the next level when we start to doubt.

People in the believing stage are often storm-tossed to-and-fro from believing to not believing as circumstances change. But once God gives that person a revelation and it is in his or her 'knower,' doubting decreases and belief grows to the next stage of knowledge.

At the knowledge level, people often think that they heard wrong and need a new message from God, when something they were hoping for doesn't come to pass right away. Often God brings a word through something we read or a person that confirms we are on track with our vision, and it causes us to not give up.

Being fully persuaded – a very important stage - is when the Word of God in your heart is truth to you, and nothing anyone says can deter you and you are inspired to continue no matter what the obstacles. Apostle Paul encouraged us to be fully persuaded as he sat in prison believing he was doing the will of God.

Commitment – the final stage – comes when there are great shakings, and it seems all is lost, but you stand in peace and know that God is on the throne. This was exemplified when Paul and Silas were on the boat in a storm that was breaking apart the ship. They knew their God would protect them and get them to their final destination.

How do we become fully persuaded? By believing that the Word of God is truth and everything else is a lie. It takes faith in the unseen – not in what we see.

In Hebrews 3:14 it says, "We are made partakers of Christ, if we hold the beginning of our confidence steadfast unto the end." God would say to you in your time of challenge and testing, "Be still and know THAT I AM GOD." (Psalm 46:10)

When I ran for schoolboard, I was fully persuaded that I was going to win. God put that in my heart. No matter what happened during the process, I know the victory was His.

My pastor asked me, "What are the odds you are going to win?" He wasn't very supportive and was inferring that it was a waste of time. I replied, "I'm not running on odds – I'm running on God's promise to me." He thought I was arrogant. But sometimes with faith, you must have confidence. When I won (by 53%), he called me an apologized for his doubt, and even apologized to his entire congregation for judging my stand of faith.

Has God put something in your heart that you believe is going to come to pass?

Prayer

Lord,

I believe in your promises, but my desire to be fully persuaded that your promises will come to pass and to not allow doubt or fear take that confidence away. Where I lack faith, give me more and bring people across my path to encourage me. I decree and declare in prayer right now, that your promises in my life will come to pass.

In Jesus' name, Amen.

Devotion #45: Praying about Job Change

"One of His disciples said to Him, 'Lord, teach us to pray...'" Luke 11:1

Prayer actually changes me more than it changes my circumstances. Often, God is more interested in working miracles in our inner nature than He is in working miracles in our external circumstances. Nowhere is the question of "prayer changing me" versus "prayer changing things" more critical than in the marketplace.

So many people I talk to are unhappy in their jobs. Sometimes God allows "needles in the nest" to cause us to take flight into new opportunities. If you haven't heard that reference before – mother birds remove the fuzzy soft feathers from the nest – a few each day – until the babies are so uncomfortable, they take flight.

However, this is not always what God is doing. Other times in challenging job experiences, God wants us to grow in the midst of our circumstances. Only prayer and time with God can help us know if we stay or fly.

John Maxwell, in his book *Life @ Work,* asks the question, Is my current career moving me toward my skill set or away from it? Maxwell reminds us that work life will not be easy with any job we take anywhere, but it is okay to evaluate if the actual job we have matches the kind of work we have been called to. (Maxwell, 2009)

Maxwell continues, "If I hold a job doing work I am good at, in an organization that is sub-par, the situation is quite different from when I am being asked to do work that I am not equipped to handle." He gives the example of Daniel being a good administrator for multiple kings over his lifetime, but for the most part, the kings themselves were cruel and oppressive.

Yet, God wanted him to stay and use his gifts.

Maxwell points out, "Daniel's job was not a fun job. God called him to work in that less-than-perfect context, yet fully prepared him to do his work with excellence," and notes, "Having fun may not be the criteria for being in the right place."

Maxwell guides us, "Ask yourself, is the tension I feel just the natural pain of God growing me in my work, or is it a symptom of a bad fit? Sometimes it is time for a job change, but sometimes I am the one who needs to be changed."

I heard Maxwell speak at a Leadership Summit in 2005, where he encouraged us by saying, "even if God is stretching you in your current job position or asking you to jump into a new job opportunity, He will ALWAYS use the gifts He gave you and not ask you to do something you are not qualified to do."

I've also learned over the years that we often have the gifts within us but we didn't know it until we were given an opportunity to use them. That's why it is important to know if God is calling you to the assignment. Spending time in prayer helps us make decisions in the marketplace.

There are several powerful stories of Christian CEOs in a book by Larry Julian titled *God Is My CEO: Following God's Principles in a Bottom-Line World (2014).* I was impressed with the stories of two CEO's who were depending on God and prayer to lead them through a tough decision. Through prayer, God gave each one the unique patience he needed.

One received patience to persevere and not let go of his plan; the other received patience to let go of his desire to climb the corporate ladder. For both, prayer was the practical tool they used to make the decision about God's will for their lives.

Prayer

Lord,

We come to you as our Creator. You designed us for a purpose. Please change the things on my job to better align with that purpose or help me see and accept the things you are doing as part of Your purpose for me. I invite you into these circumstances to show me a new path or reveal to me what training or preparation I am in right now. I trust you with my life.

In Jesus' name, Amen.

Devotion #46: Soar Like an Eagle

"Blessed are the poor in spirit..." (Matthew 5:3)

"Poor in spirit" means admitting that we are unable to do the task. When we admit that we cannot, that is when God rejoices, because He gets it done through us.

It is in those moments we proclaim, "I can do all things through Christ which strengthens me" (Philippians 4:13). An evangelist/pastor once said to me, "You feel totally empty right now after two years of doing nothing. Great! Now God can fill you with Himself because there is nothing of you left!"

When I meditate on what the possibilities are for the next level of leadership, I truly feel inadequate and unprepared for the task. Yet, going into the unknown or a new level of skill and growth is usually God's will for our lives. The God-given gifts, talents, and strengths are within us. The job assignments develop those into leadership skills and character.

When we feel poor in the spirit in our waiting season, we can be assured that when it is His time, He will fill us with Himself, and we will be able to give Him all the glory for how He has equipped us. In the end, it will be all about Him, not about us.

I once heard a story about a baby eagle raised by a farmer along with his chickens. When it came time for the eagle to soar, he thought he was a chicken and would not fly. When tossed from the top of the barn by the farmer, he would return to the earth to enjoy eating the chicken feed with his peers. The farmer finally took him to a mountaintop and tossed him in the air, and he soared.

Ephesians 3:20 says, "Now to Him who, by the power that is at work within us, is able to (carry out His purpose and) do superabundantly, far over and above all that we (dare) ask or think (infinitely beyond our highest prayers, desires, thoughts, hopes or dreams)."

Are you waiting on God for His purpose in your life? Remember, if He calls you, it means he equipped you with the potential, gifts, and talents to succeed. Step out in faith and start to soar.

Prayer

Lord,

I don't always feel fully equipped to do all the things you require of me. But I trust you have prepared me for my assignments and where I am weak you are strong. My desire is to do your will. Please give me peace and assurance as I step into a new role or take on new responsibilities. Thank you.

In Jesus' name, Amen.

Devotion #47: Waiting Versus Walking

"But those who wait on the Lord... shall walk and not faint." (Isaiah 40:31 NKJV)

Since I love variety and change, I believe that walking is better than waiting. However, the greatest growth in my life came through waiting upon God not moving forward in my own strength and timing.

When we wait, we are keeping the Lord before us, keeping our eyes on Him, and staying "tuned" to the next direction. Waiting keeps us from getting ahead of the Lord and allows for His perfect timing and His highest will to be accomplished in our lives and in others.

In waiting we learn to understand the reality of God's presence. We learn to trust Him based on His Word, not on our experiences. Everyone's waiting experiences are different. Some wait to conceive a child; others wait for a new job opportunity; and others wait for a healing from loss, rejection, or grief.

Without the growth of waiting, how would we ever get to a state of mind and heart of Psalm 6:2-3: "We will not fear, though the earth be removed, and though the mountains be carried into the midst of the sea; though the waters thereof roar and be troubled, though the mountains shake."

The wilderness experiences test our trust in God and cause us to wait upon Him. If we abide in Him, walk before Him (listening carefully), and trust the reality of His presence in our lives, we can make everyday decisions with confidence.

In 1984, God led me to wait before Him in His Word for 18 months until He gave me the next direction for my life. Toward the end of the phase, I confessed to a friend that I felt useless and that I was doing nothing for the kingdom of God or for my life.

She told me that the "waiting" was so powerful that the enemy wanted to discourage me and stop it because the strength and wisdom of the Lord was going down deep in my spirit. I proceeded to continue to wait with a little more interest in the process.

A short time later, I was called to run for school board and to a nationwide traveling/lobbying ministry. The stories of leaders in the Bible and the messages of Psalm and Proverbs I had read over those 18 months, now became the sword and shield I needed to survive. After a long wait, I suddenly turned into an eagle in full flight carried by the winds of God in a fulltime mission for Him.

What is the difference between the eagle and other birds? Birds all fly flapping their wings, but the eagle soars, allowing the wind to carry her.

Isaiah 40:31 says: "But they that wait upon the Lord shall renew their strength; they shall mount up with wings as eagles; they shall run, and not be weary; they shall walk, and not faint."

Prayer

Lord,

Help me to continue to put my trust in you and not get discouraged during my waiting season. Seal to my heart that waiting is good for me and that you are using this time to allow my roots to go down deep to prepare for the "suddenly" (the sudden answer to prayer) that will take me to high places. I put my life in your hands and expect good things to come.

In Jesus' name, Amen.

Can God Come to Work with Me?

Devotion #48: God's Purpose for Your Life

"And I will give you the treasurers of darkness and hidden riches of secret places, that you may know that it is I, the Lord, the God of Israel, Who calls you by your name." (Isaiah 45:3)

Did you know that God's purpose for your life is not impacted by your circumstances? Your circumstances mean nothing to what He has planned for you.

God's promises for you are not altered one bit by the fact that you may have spent half your life in sin; that you married too young; or that you got saved late in life. There is absolutely nothing that God cannot handle and absolutely nothing that can stop the hand of God.

When you think about God's calling on your life, do not let the term "missionary" deter you from receiving God's direction. We are all missionaries wherever we serve, called to be examples for Christ.

As the world gets darker and the pressures get greater, people are watching the strength, peace, and joy that rest upon us. At some point, like moths, they will be drawn to that light, because they desperately need it.

The Bible is not a textbook of doctrine – it is a textbook of people's stories and lives. It is a book of stories of men and women who walked with God. It's about character and wisdom. You have a story too – but it will not be written in the Book of Life unless you start living your story to the fullest.

What is the real point of our existence? Jesus boiled it all down to two things: loving God and loving others. Do this, He said, and you will find the purpose of your life. Everything else will fall into place.

Find what your talent is and give it to the world. Because of your love toward God, you have a special assignment to give God's love to others. Everything you need is in your heart.

Your mission is simply sharing your life message, living a life for Christ, keeping your life in balance, using your gifts and talents, and living with a purpose.

The next time you see the word "missions," don't think about China and Africa (unless God is calling you there) – think about the marketplace you are in right now, and let God's strength, peace, love, and joy flow out to others right where you are.

Executive coach John Maxwell asks, "Are you fighting for the individuals where you work (or in your neighborhood), or do you just pass them by in the hall (or on the street)?"

He reminds us that people all around us are stripped of their self-confidence, self-worth, hope, faith, purity, meaning, and opportunity. They are abandoned, lonely, gripped by fear and doubt.

If we just get to know them, we will discover their hurt and need. There is a sign over the inside of my office door that I read as I go to teach my classes. It says "Now entering the mission field."

Prayer

Lord,

Thank you for reminding me that my workplace is my mission place. I often think there may be something more important for me to do. But the people you put in our sphere, in our path, on our team, in the classroom, are the most important. Help me to be more sensitive to what you want to do through me for others or say to others. I'm available, Lord. I'm listening.

In Jesus' name, Amen.

Devotion #49: God Guards Our Lives

"For He will give His angels charge concerning you, to guard you in all your ways." (Psalm 91:11)

God wants us to draw on His grace in prayer, and He wants us to invite Him into every situation. God will also deliver you and keep you safe from danger when you least expect it.

In the mid-1970s, I was in a pole yard in Seattle learning how to climb telephone poles. It was graduation day, and I wanted to go home to my family.

We were told that if we ever "cut out" (that is, if little metal points, called gaffs, on the straps attached to our boots broke away from the pole) we were not to "hug" the pole or we would slide all the way down, and our bodies would be full of splinters. Even at 18 feet in the air, we were told that our best chance of painless survival was to fall to the ground.

We were also told that if we ever "cut out," we would be set back two weeks in the training. On my last morning, I was practicing for the final test.

The phone company required us to go up and down the pole without a belt, only depending on our gaffs. We only belted in when we were working at the top.

On my last practice run, without a belt, I cut out at the 18-foot height. Even though they said not to, I instinctively hugged the pole and amazingly did not move. I looked at the instructors and their backs were to me on the other side of the pole yard.

I quickly asked God for help and whispered, "Jesus, what should I do?" Talk about a grace prayer! I suddenly became aware of what felt like two hands under my bottom-side holding me up like a platform.

A still small voice said, "Release one leg at a time from the pole and place your gaffs into the pole until you are secure."

In the natural, if I had released one leg from the "death grip" it had on that pole, I would have fallen, but my faith was in what God was telling me. I slowly got secured back into the pole while God kept the instructors distracted for what seemed like an eternity, and I "gaffed" my way back down the pole.

Eventually the instructors came over and said, "Are you ready to show us your last climb?" Amazingly I had no fear and quickly demonstrated my final climb and graduated.

I found out when I arrived home that a sister-in-the-Lord, while doing dishes at 9:00 a.m., suddenly thought about me and prayed with a sense of urgency. That was the exact time I needed an angel. The fact that God asked someone to pray for me continues to affirm that God hears our prayers.

I know this may be an extreme workplace story and you will probably not be on a phone pole anytime soon, but there could be an emergency, and I want to encourage you with the message, God will be there for you.

Prayer

Lord,

I thank you for demonstrating your faithfulness to hear my prayer and putting on someone's heart to pray for me. I pray for my readers that in that same hour they need you, they will remember this amazing story and know that you will deliver them from any danger or frightening circumstances. Thank you for your promise that the angels watch over us and for your protection always.

In Jesus' name, Amen.

Devotion #50: Spiritual Muscles

"In the world ye shall have tribulation: but be of good cheer; I have overcome the world." (John 16:33)

When I moved to Palm Desert, CA, to take a job at a community college, I had to come eighteen months ahead of my husband while we waited for his retirement.

My job started on August 10, 1999, and on August 2, 1999 I have recorded in my journal where I asked the Lord, "Why does it have to be so hard? Other families relocate together."

My journal notes continued: "The last mission you called me on in Washington, D.C. we were separated then, too. Why do we have to be separated again? Are you sure we are doing the right thing?"

I looked up what I wrote during the WA DC challenge, and it said: "God does not help us overcome life, He gives us life as we overcome. In our strain is actually our strength."

I began to laugh and cry at the same time and wrote in my journal a second time: "Of course this move is a strain! Of course, this seems impossible for me! Because you want me to depend on you! You want me to know you even more! You want to show me how You are my provider and how You are going to take care of every detail, give me favor, and give me strength."

During this time of preparation to move, I called my daughter who lived in Texas and shared with her how I was getting the strength to leave for my new job in a few days. I said to her, "I wonder what would have happened if I said 'no' when God asked me to run for school board? I wonder where I would be today if I said 'no' to living in Washington, D.C.? I wonder what would have happened if I said 'no' regarding getting my education? If I said 'no' to all those things, I would not be facing this decision right now."

My daughter replied, "Mommy" – she still called me Mommy – "I wouldn't be who I am today if you said 'no' to God. Because of the example you set, I had the courage to go to college and trust God to pay for it. I had the courage to leave home and come to Texas to teach. Look at all the good things that are happening to me in Texas. I'm growing in my Spanish language; I have a good job, and I met my husband. You influenced me so much, and my life is so much better because you said 'yes' to God."

God richly blessed me with those words. Every time I face new stretches and stresses, the timing brings me back to this devotion and these words of encouragement.

An evangelist once said, "Without pressure and resistance, we cannot build spiritual muscles." I can assure you from experience, that the pressure is not forever, and when you get to the other side of these circumstances, you will have developed spiritual muscles for the next phase of your life – actually, for the rest of your life.

Prayer

Lord,

I praise you for all the stretches and challenges I went through over my working lifetime so that I can encourage my listeners that you are a good and faithful God. That with you, nothing is impossible. And with You, all things work together for those who love the Lord and in accordance with His purpose. As Jesus asked you to be with his disciples as they remained in the world, I ask You to be with my readers and they follow you and your teachings in the workplace.

In Jesus' name, Amen.

About the Author

Dr. Wendy Flint, author and international speaker, has over 35-years' experience in the business sector and higher education. From elected official, to supervisor and manager, to corporate executive, to higher education administrator, she has achieved her goals with faith and grit. She is author of 10 books and training manuals for business, government, education, and faith-based audiences.

Wendy has a compassion for men and women incarcerated in prison and believes education and Jesus is the way to change lives. She served as an ordained minister through Kairos Ministry in Texas for four years.

Wendy and her husband Terry of over 50 years, met and married while both serving in the U.S. Navy during the Vietnam War. They later served together in the Portland Air National Guard and were both trained in telecommunications. Pacific NW Bell hired them on the same day as the first married couple hired for lineman positions. Terry retired from the phone company after 26 years.

Terry and Wendy reside in Sherwood, Oregon and have three children and six grandchildren.

Dr. Flint holds an AA in Administration of Justice (Clark College), a BA in Communication with a Specialization in Corporate Training (Marylhurst University), Masters of Public Administration (Washington State University), Masters of Business Administration (Capella University), and a PhD in Education with a Specialization in Teaching and Learning (Capella University).

You can follow Wendy at
www.wendyflint.com
www.linkedin.com/in/drwendyflint
www.facebook.com/marketplacechristians

Can God Come to Work with Me?

Other Books by Dr. Wendy Flint

Women of Purpose: Live the Life You Were Born to Live (Amazon)

Workplace Prayers (Amazon)

Prison Prayers (Amazon)

MarketplaceChristians.com (Amazon)

Problem-based Learning: Welcome to the Real World (Amazon)

Principled and Practical Leadership (Training Manual)

Teaching Techniques for Adult Learners (Training Manual)

School Boards – A Call to Action (2nd Edition to be released 2022)

Teaching Employability (To be released 2022)

Podcasts

These devotions have been recorded in 50 Podcasts and are located at Spotify, Apple, and other Podcast platforms.

Go to wendyflint.com for more detailed information.

Can God Come to Work with Me?

References

Brooks, P. (2007). THE PURPOSE AND USE OF COMFORT (SERMONS BY A 19TH CENTURY, EPISCOPALIAN BISHOP. Cosmo Classics.

Brown, B. (2018). DARE TO LEAD: BRAVE WORK. TOUGH CONVERSATIONS. WHOLE HEARTS. Random House.

Chewning, R.C., Eby, J.W., & Rolls, S.J. (1990). BUSINESS THROUGH THE EYES OF FAITH. HarperOne.

Chambers, O. (Year of 1992). MY UTMOST FOR HIS HIGHEST. Discovery House Publishers.

Collins, J. (2000). GOOD TO GREAT: WHY SOME COMPANIES MAKE THE LEAP . . . AND OTHERS DON'T. HarperCollins Publishers.

Copeland, G. & Copeland, K. (1991). FROM FAITH TO FAITH: A DAILY GUIDE TO VICTORY. KCM.

Julian, L. (2014). GOD IS MY CEO: FOLLOWING GOD'S PRINCIPLES IN A BOTTOM-LINE WORLD, 2nd Edition. Simon & Shuster, Inc.

Maxwell, J. C. (2005). LIFE@WORK: MARKETPLACE SUCCESS FOR PEOPLE OF FAITH. Thomas Nelson.

Maxwell, J. (2019). NIV, MAXWELL LEADERSHIP BIBLE, 3RD EDITION. Thomas Nelson.

Smith, M.W. (2019). AWAKEN: THE SURROUNDED EXPERIENCE (AUDIO CD). Rocketown Records.

Wilkinson, B. (2005). THE PRAYER OF JABEZ: BREAKING THROUGH TO A BLESSED LIFE. Multnomah Books.

Wilkinson, B. (2006). SECRETS OF THE VINE: BREAKING THROUGH TO ABUNDANCE. Multnomah Books.

Ziglar, Z. (2020). GOALS: HOW TO GET THE MOST OUT OF YOUR LIFE. Nightingale Conant.

Made in USA - Kendallville, IN
82239_9780981847023
08.27.2022 1356